THE
FAERYLAND
COMPANION

THE
FAERYLAND
COMPANION

Beatrice Phillpotts

PAVILION

First published in Great Britain in 1999 by
PAVILION BOOKS LIMITED
London House, Great Eastern Wharf
Parkgate Road, London SW11 4NQ

Edited and designed by Ash & Higton
Designed by Bernard Higton
Project Management by Russell Ash

A CIP catalogue record for this book is available
from the British Library

ISBN 1 86205 120 8

Set in Cochin and Caslon Antique
Printed in Hong Kong by Imago
Colour origination by DP Reprographics Limited, England

2 4 6 8 10 9 7 5 3 1

This book can be ordered direct from the publisher. Please contact
the Marketing Department. But try your bookshop first.

CONTENTS

The COMING of the FAERIES

THE FAERIES are as eternal as the human beings who created them. A belief in faeries has always existed, although it has meant something different to each generation.

The word 'faery' originally came from the Latin 'fatae', meaning the Fates. It also meant 'faerie', a state of enchantment, which could be either a place or the spirits who lived there.

Faerie was described in the seventeenth century as one species of supernatural creatures 'of a middle nature between man and angel'. The word is now more commonly used to cover the whole area of the supernatural not claimed by angels and devils, and the name 'faeries' or fairies is recognized everywhere.

In British folklore, faery embraces a huge cast of characters ranging from the familiar elves, dragons and mermaids to the more rarefied seal-like Selkies, the monstrous Irish Firbolgs and the Scottish spinner Habetrots. The word is also used to describe a number of spirits with similar characteristics, who reappear in tales from all over Britain, under different names according to the area in which they live. The Brownie, for example, is the Bwca in Wales, the Bodach in the Highlands and the Fenodoree in the Isle of Man.

To mention the faery name, either individually or collectively, however, was originally considered taboo by many people. The restriction probably stemmed from the primitive belief that to name a person, or spirit, is to have power over them. The earliest faeries of folk legend represented powerful natural forces that were to be feared and placated. Their love of secrecy was respected by those anxious not to offend them and they were described, euphemistically, as 'the Good Neighbours' or 'the Good Folk'.

The earliest written reference to faeries of any kind in England, occurs in an eleventh-century manuscript of Anglo-Saxon charms against elf-shot. This was a magic, disease-bearing arrow used by elves to harm their unfortunate victims.

When oral tales of faery beliefs and faery sightings started to be written down, a wealth of folk legend was available for writers and artists to draw upon. Later, as belief in them declined, the faeries became more decorative than monstrous and today's popular image of faeryland was largely shaped by the captivating miniature world imagined by Shakespeare in *A Midsummer Night's Dream*. Its faery scenes have influenced generations of writers and artists.

Faery Theories

The following theories have been advanced by folklorists to explain the coming of the faeries:

The Hades Theory *Faeries are the souls of the unforgiven dead, waiting to be reunited with their bodies at Judgement Day.*

The Mythological Theory *Faeries are the diminished figures of the old pagan Celtic divinities.*

The Pigmy Theory *Faeries derive from a folk memory of a prehistoric Mongolian race, which inhabited Britain and parts of Europe but died out after its members were driven out by the Celts.*

The Druid Theory *Faeries derive from a folk memory of the Druids and their magical practices.*

The Naturalistic Theory *Faeries are a continuation of a prehistoric belief in nature spirits.*

The Psychological Theory *Faeries are the manifestation of a worldwide doctrine of souls, and part of the universal animistic spirit.*

The Actual Theory *Faeries are a real race of supernatural beings.*

INTO the UNDERWORLD

FAERYLAND is most commonly thought of as being situated underground, which links it firmly with ideas of the Underworld and the lands of the Dead.

Hades, the mythical underworld ruled over by Pluto the Greek god of the dead, was frequently confused with faeryland. The fourteenth-century English poet Chaucer described Pluto as 'Kyng of fayrie', and in his *Merchant's Tale* tells of his wife 'Proserpine and all her fayrie'; and a character in an old Scottish play, Philotus, cries out 'gang hence to hell or to the Faerie'.

If any food or drink was consumed by a living visitor while they were in Hades, they were compelled to remain there forever. A similar taboo exists in faeryland. When the Celtic St Collen visited a faery palace in Glastonbury Tor, Somerset, he took drastic measures to avoid joining the banquet that was in progress. When the faery king begged him to eat and drink with them, St Collen flatly refused. He told the faeries to go to Hell and threw a concealed flask of holy water over the assembly, at which both palace and faeries instantly vanished.

The subterranean faeryland recalls not only Hades but also the dead that are buried underground. Prehistoric barrows (the heaps of earth that were placed over tombs) were often believed to house faery palaces. In Ireland the chiefs of the faery people were believed to have ruled from the Bronze Age burial

mound known as the Brugh of the Boyne.

According to folk legend, mortals could gain entry into the subterranean faery regions in a variety of different ways: in parts of Scotland access to a hollow faery hill might be granted by circling it nine times, at which point a door would open; Cliach, a famous Irish harpist, entered the faery hill of the elf king Bedb by playing his harp nearby until the ground opened up – his music had made him welcome in faeryland.

Traditionally, human fertility has been closely linked with that of the earth. According to popular belief, however, the association of the faeries with the dead was far more negative. They were widely regarded as fearful spirits who took much of their strength from the living. Faery activity was always feared most at times of human or agricultural fertility. If 'the Good Neighbours' were angry, they could ruin your crops or make your wife barren.

Einion goes Underground

'One day when it was cloudy and misty, a shepherd boy going to the mountains lost his way and walked about for hours. At last he came to a hollow place surrounded by rushes where he saw a number of round rings. He recognized the place as one he had often heard of as being dangerous for shepherds, because of the rings. He tried to get away from there but he could not. Then an old, merry, blue-eyed man appeared. The boy thinking to find his way home, followed him and the old man said, "Do not speak a word till I tell you."

In a little while they came to a menhir [standing stone]. The old man tapped it three times and then lifted it up. A narrow path with steps descending was revealed and from it emerged a bluish-white light. "Follow me," said the old man, "no harm will come to you". The boy did so and it was not long before he saw a fine, wooded, fertile country with a beautiful palace and rivers and mountains. He reached the palace and was enchanted by the singing of birds. Music of all sorts was in the palace but he saw no people. At meals, dishes came and disappeared of their own accord. He could hear voices all about him but saw no person except the old man – who said that now he could speak. When he tried to speak he found that he could not move his tongue.

Soon a smiling old lady came to him, leading three beautiful maidens and when the maidens saw the shepherd boy they smiled and spoke but he could not reply. Then one of the girls kissed him, and all at once he began to converse freely and most wittily. He lived with the maidens in the palace a year and a day, in full enjoyment of the marvellous country, not thinking it more than a day, for there was no reckoning of time in that land.'

From an ancient
Welsh legend

BENEATH the DEEP

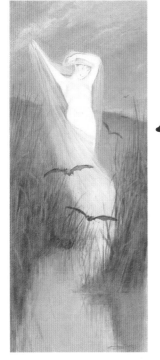

At times faeryland was thought to be 'over the seas and far away'. The ancient Irish believed in a beautiful country beyond the sea, known as the Land of Promise, that was inhabited by gods and sometimes visited by heroes. This overseas Elysium gradually metamorphosed into becoming an alternative faeryland. The faery race, Tuatha de Danann, could be found under the tumuli of prehistoric Ireland, or in Tirfo Thuinn, the Land under the Waves.

In an attempt to explain the co-existence of two faery otherworlds, the British nineteenth-century folklorist Alfred Nutt suggested that they came from two strains of belief arising from co-existing cultures. One launched its dead warriors to their resting places upon the western sea, the other buried its dead in great mounds.

The idea that there is an overseas faery paradise owes its existence to mythological stories of Avalon, the Island of the Blessed. Medieval romances are full of heroes who have been bewitched by faery women and lured to the kingdom of Avalon. King Arthur retired there to heal his wounds, and his knights Sir Launcelot and Sir Gawain also visited it.

J. R. R. Tolkien concluded his great trilogy *The Lord of the Rings* with the departure of the elves of Middle Earth by ship from the Grey Havens out into the High Sea towards 'white shores and beyond them a far green country under a swift sunrise'.

Although it was always remote, this faery Elysium was not necessarily thought to be across the ocean. Lakes were also a popular location. According to Celtic legend, Laeghaire, son of the king of Connaught, and fifty of his warriors, plunged into a lake to assist a faery man who had begged for help in recovering his wife, kidnapped by an underwater rival. An underwater faery enchantress, The Lady of the Lake, is well known from Arthurian legend.

The nineteenth-century folklorist, Lady Wilde, the mother of Oscar Wilde, described the faeries of Lough Neagh in Ireland:

'Deep down, under the waters of Lough Neagh, can still be seen, by those who have the gift of fairy vision, the columns and walls of the beautiful palaces once inhabited by the fairy race when they were gods of the earth; and this tradition of a buried town beneath the waves has been prevalent for centuries among the people.'

An ENGLISH WOOD near ATHENS

THE FAERY WORLD at the heart of the English countryside that William Shakespeare portrayed in *A Midsummer Night's Dream* is the most potent evocation of faeryland ever written. It is also the first play in which the faery theme is treated extensively.

The dramatic action might officially be set in classical Greece, but Shakespeare's magical 'wood near Athens', the faeryland of the play, has an extremely English aspect. He describes the familiar beauty of his native landscape. The flowers decorating his faery kingdom were 'cowslips tall', 'luscious woodbine', 'nodding violets' and 'sweet musk-roses', and the faery queen Titania's tiny followers were identified so closely with them that they bore names such as Peaseblossom and Mustardseed.

Shakespeare not only made his faeries deliberately tiny – for almost the first time in literature – but they were also generally benevolent. Titania's miniature helpers drove away the owl, snake, spiders, newts and bats, all of whom are creatures associated with witchcraft, and she was concerned that her quarrel with the faery king, Oberon, would create problems for the human world.

Shakespeare's miniaturized faeryland and his concentration on its decorative delights provided a new, imaginative perspective that inspired generations of writers and artists and helped to shape our contemporary image of faeryland. The faery from the play who 'must go seek some dewdrops here, and hang a pearl in every cowslip's ear' is a direct ancestor of twentieth-century artist Cecily Mary Barker's delicately detailed flower faeries that are so popular today.

Shakespeare owed a debt both to classical mythology and to folk tradition in the creation of his faery characters in *A Midsummer Night's Dream*. Folklore gave him the characters Puck or Robin Goodfellow, the domestic hobgoblin with a roving eye and a penchant for mischief-making. However, in place of Mab, the earthy faery queen of popular legend, he substituted the more courtly Titania, who has many attributes of the goddess Diana.

Shakespeare's faeries in *A Midsummer Night's Dream* may be small but they can be formidable. They control the weather and the seasons, and when they quarrel all Nature goes awry. His knowledge of country beliefs inspired the faeries portrayed in other plays, although they were never again as central to the action. His Queen Mab in *Romeo and Juliet* has a number of elfin qualities. She is a tiny faery, who departs from tradition by driving a hazel-nut carriage pulled by ants. In *The Tempest* the airy faery Ariel is a type of nature spirit.

The tiny, flowery faeryland of Shakespeare's *A Midsummer Night's Dream* has had a lasting influence. A cult of the miniature sprang up in the seventeenth century, in which poets vied to create yet more fanciful images of a faery lifestyle at the heart of nature. A fashion for faery painting developed in the nineteenth century, and scenes from *A Midsummer Night's Dream* proved the most popular source of inspiration.

Faery paintings by the British artist William Blake helped to launch the trend. They were inspired by Shakespeare but were also influenced by traditional country beliefs. Blake believed in faeries and described seeing 'a procession of creatures the size and colour of green and grey grasshoppers, bearing a body laid out on a rose-leaf' while walking alone in his garden.

Shakespeare's faeries and the Victorian stage

A Midsummer Night's Dream *was extremely popular in the nineteenth-century theatre, and no expense was spared in the creation of ever more dazzling effects. The difficulties of achieving a dream-like state of mind among spectators was overcome by making actors appear and disappear with the use of trapdoors, sliding platforms and gauzes. Flying machinery was used to help sustain the faery illusion.*

An 1853 production at Sadler's Wells Theatre, London, by Samuel Phelps was praised by the contemporary critic Henry Morley for its spell-binding special effects. Commenting on the introduction of coloured gauze, he wrote: 'It subdued the flesh and blood of the actors into something more nearly resembling dream-like figures, and incorporated more completely the actors with the scenes, throwing the same green fairy tinge, and the same mist over all.'

Faery elves, whose midnight revels by a forest-side,
Or fountain, some belated peasant sees,
Or dreams he sees, while overhead the Moon
Sits arbitress and nearer to the Earth
Wheels her pale course, they on their mirth and dance
Intent, with jocund music charm his ear;
At once with joy and fear his heart rebounds.

FROM *PARADISE LOST* BY JOHN MILTON

J. R. R. Tolkien in *The Lord of the Rings*, first published in one volume in 1968, memorably described the Hobbits' first meeting with a venerable tree spirit, named Treebeard: 'A large Man-like, almost Troll-like, figure, at least fourteen foot high, very sturdy, with a tall head, and hardly any neck. Whether it was clad in stuff like green and grey bark, or whether that was its hide, was difficult to say. At any rate the arms, at a short distance from the trunk, were not wrinkled, but covered with a sweeping grey beard, bushy, almost twiggy at the roots, thin and mossy at the ends. But at the moment the hobbits noted little but the eyes. These deep eyes were now surveying them, shot with a green light.'

ENCHANTED TREES

Cults of tree worship pre-date Christianity. Attempts were made by the Church to eradicate such pagan beliefs but they continued to flourish, notably in faery mythology.

Nearly all trees have some sacred association, dating back to ancient beliefs and the custom of tree burial. Faeries, like the dead, were believed to inhabit trees. According to legend, the soul of the dead was believed to pass into the tree, where it awaited re-incarnation.

Folklore is full of warnings of the dangers of cutting trees or bushes known to be haunted by faeries. In some cases, the act proved impossible. An attempt by foresters in Ulster to chop down a 'skiough', or faery bush, resulted in their hatchet breaking. If mortals persevered, however, and felled a faery tree, they were persecuted by bad luck for the rest of their lives.

The spirit of the hawthorn was apt to be vindictive if it was cut or interfered with in any way. The cattle of a farmer who demolished a hawthorn perished and his children died one by one, while two Irish brothers who felled hawthorns on a burial mound 'lost their luck' – indeed, one was 'faery struck so badly nothing would cure him'.

The hawthorn tree was traditionally the tree of the Faery Queen. It was considered unlucky to bring flowering hawthorn inside, as it would bring death to the house. The thirteenth-century Scottish landowner, Thomas the Rhymer, who was believed to have vanished into Faeryland for seven years, warned neighbouring villagers to look after their hawthorn well:

> As long as the Thorn Tree stands
> Erceldoune shall keep its lands.

The tree, known as the Eildon Tree, remained standing until as late as 1814, when it was blown over in a storm. The villagers tried to revive it by pouring whisky over its roots, but to no avail. The prophecy proved correct. The village was struck by a chain of financial disasters and it had to sell off its commonland to pay its debts.

Into the scented woods we'll go,
And see the blackthorn swim in snow.
High above, in the budding leaves,
A brooding dove awakes and grieves;
The glades with mingled music stir,
And wildly laughs the woodpecker.
When blackthorn petals pearl the breeze,
There are the twisted hawthorne trees
Thick-set with buds, as clear and pale
As golden water or green hail —
As if a storm of rain had stood
Enchanted in the thorny wood,
And, hearing fairy voices call,
Hung poised, forgetting how to fall.

MARY WEBB, *GREEN RAIN*

A well-known folk rhyme maintained 'Faery folks are in old oaks'. The oak was worshipped by the Druids and it had strong magical associations. The children's writer Beatrix Potter mentioned the mischievous faery Oakmen, a squat, dwarfish people with red toadstool caps and red noses in *The Faery Caravan*. Ruth Tongue's *Forgotten Folk-Tales of the English Counties* relates the story of a hunted vixen that was saved by the Oakmen, 'who guard all forest beasts'. They pulled her safely inside their tree and healed her wounds, saying, "Wipe your sore paws in our oaktree rainpool." So she did and her coat grew again and her pads were healed.

Bad luck could be averted in the case of an elder tree, according to Lincolnshire legend, if permission to cut it was first requested of the faeries. One local explained, 'You just says: "Owd Gal, give me of they wood and Oi will give some of moine when I grows inter a tree".'

FLOWERY DELIGHTS

CERTAIN FLOWERS offered powerful protection against faery enchantment, according to folk legend. The best known of these was a four-leafed clover, a plant still widely regarded as bringing good luck. A magic ointment that made faeries visible was said to be made from four-leafed clover, as a milkmaid discovered in a folk tale included in *Popular Romances of the West of England* by Robert Hunt:

'There was a most beautiful cow called Daisy in a farm at West Buriens, who was in milk for long seasons with a splendid quality of milk, but she never let down more than two gallons, then she would prick her ears forward, give a soft low and hold back her milk. One evening a milkmaid was milking the cows in the meadow when this happened. She put a pad of grass on her head to soften the weight of the pail, picked up the pail and started for home. As she crossed the stile she glanced back at Daisy and saw that she was surrounded by fairies, who swarmed over her with little pipkins [pots] in their hands. They patted and stroked her, and Daisy was clearly delighted with their company. One rather bigger than the rest, whom she recognized as a pixy by his impudent grin, was lying on his back with his feet in the air, and the others took turns in standing on them to milk the cow.'

The milkmaid discovered that she had included a four-leafed clover in her grass pad that had made the faeries visible.

St John's wort (*Hypericum*) was another plant believed to have power over the faeries. It was carried by country folk as a charm to keep faeries away, a practice noted by Sir Walter Scott, who tells of the following rhyme that was spoken by a demon who could not approach a girl because she was carrying St John's wort and verbena:

If you would be true love mine,
Throw away John's wort and Verbein.

Some plants, in particular the foxglove, cow's parsley, water lily and dock had special properties that could cure anyone cursed with a 'faery stroke' – that was an evil enchantment that could cause paralysis. However, extreme caution had to be used when applying such a remedy, because it could bring on another attack.

The perils of lily of the valley were well known and are illustrated in a Somerset folk song:

The Lily she grows in the greenwood,
Maidens, maidens take care!
Her sweet-scented breath do tell of your death,
Maidens, beware.

The warning was disregarded by one foolish woman, according to a Sussex legend. She sent her daughter to pick some, '…so of course the little girl sickened and died, as everyone knew she would'. The little girl,

Of leaves of Roses white and red,
Shall be the Covering of her bed:
The Curtaines, Valence, Tester, all,
Shall be the flower Imperiall,
And for the Fringe, it all along
With azure Harebels shall be hung:
Of Lillies shall the Pillowes be,
With downe stuft of the Butterflee.

FROM *NYMPHIDIA* BY MICHAEL DRAYTON

however, had made her mother promise
to lay a bunch on her coffin, before she
died. The woman was unable to find any
but came across 'an old man all in black',
who handed her a basket of lilies of the
valley. 'She never knew where he came
from or where he went, and nobody else
had seen him before.' The mother was
able to keep the promise she had made
to her dying daughter, and put the
flowers on the coffin, but she died
herself three days later.

As popular belief in the fearsome
faeries of folk legend declined, flowers
became a decorative adornment for
miniature faerylands. The faery King
Oberon's delightful description of his
queen Titania's flowery bower in *A
Midsummer Night's Dream* inspired a
fresh vision of faeryland:

I know a bank where the wild thyme blows,
Where oxlips and the nodding violet grows,
Quite over-canopied with luscious woodbine,
With sweet musk-roses, and with eglantine.

As the faeries diminished in size, they became
more closely identified with their surrounding
plant world.

Earlier folk beliefs about particular plants
were forgotten. No longer considered a powerful
charm against the faeries, the foxglove became a
popular faery hat, while lilies served as faery

pillows. The imaginative potential of a tiny,
flowery faery world, received its best known
recent expression in Cicely Mary Barker's *The
Book of the Flower Fairies, and Flower Fairies of the
Garden*. Her detailed illustrations have delighted
generations of children and are still enormously
popular. However, she was careful to distance
herself from the miniature nature spirits she
wrote about, and admits in her preface: 'I have
never seen a faery, the faeries and all about them
are just pretend.'

MAGIC MUSHROOMS

THE MUSHROOM, traditionally thought of as the spawn of the gods, became a favourite faery prop, whether it was as a throne, a banqueting table or part of a faery ring – but it was a relatively recent addition to faeryland.

Folklore is full of references to the midnight ring danced around by the faeries, and many attempts have been made to explain the circles of withered or bright green grass around which the faeries were believed to dance.

These rings have been attributed to a species of mushroom, *Agaricus pratinus*, which propagates by sending out a network of threads that frequently form a circular shape. The way in which fungi apparently spring out of nowhere and grow with such speed also gave the species a suitably magical aura. By the end of the nineteenth century, illustrations of faeries dancing generally showed mushrooms somewhere in the picture.

The poisonous nature of the toadstool, the name popularly given to inedible mushrooms, gave sinister overtones to faery revels, while the hallucinogenic properties of the fly agaric, or magic mushroom, made its appearance in faeryland even more appropriate. The toadstool, like the toad, is believed to represent the sacred mushroom that gives enlightenment.

Shakespeare did not mention mushrooms as part of the faery habitat but the Jacobean poets were quick to realize its imaginative potential in their search for suitable decorations in their miniature faery worlds.

In *The Pastime and Recreation of the Queen of the Fairies in Fairyland, the Centre of the Earth*, the Duchess of Newcastle wrote about Queen Mab's lifestyle in elaborate detail. The faery queen dined from a mushroom table spread with a cobweb and feasted on 'Amelets made of Ants-eggs new…her milk from the Dormouse udder.'

The popular image of a cross-legged pixie seated on a toadstool, now seen most often as a garden ornament, comes from the fanciful descriptions of the Jacobean poets, which in turn inspired the artists of the late eighteenth and nineteenth centuries. Sir Joshua Reynolds appears to have started the trend in 1789 with a painting of Puck that showed the fairy as an impish baby sitting on a mushroom. It was a very popular composition. When the painting was sold at auction, it 'excited such admiration that there was a general clapping of hands'.

Another faery composition, *Titania's Awakening*, by Henry Fuseli, shows the

It ganne to rayne, the kinge and Queene they runne
Under a mushroom fretted over head
With Glowormes, Artificially doune,
Resembling much the canopy of a bedd
Of cloth of silver: and such glimmeringe light
It gave, as stars doe in a frosty night.

FROM A JACOBEAN POEM *THE SPORTS OF THE FAIRIES*

faery king and queen and members of their court on a mushroom. Subsequent faery painters also featured the mushroom prominently. In Richard Dadd's *Puck*, the elf is seated cross-legged on a spotlit mushroom, with faeries performing a frenzied dance around him.

In an erotic faery scene painted by Thomas Heatherley, *Fairy Seated on a Mushroom*, a nude miniature Venus is seated with her back to the viewer on the phallic shape of the mushroom, its fleshy curves mirrored by her own. In Heatherley's *Fairy Resting on a Mushroom*, which he painted at the same time, a tiny faery odalisque is draped across a mushroom, surrounded by menacing spiky demons.

Echoes of Jacobean descriptions of mushroom banqueting tables linger in John Anster Fitzgerald's visionary scenes of faeryland. He painted several faery feasts, each of which have a sinister edge to them. In *The Fairies Banquet*, the narcotic purple convolvulus hangs over the meal, showing that the food is not good for mortals to eat. The fact that the delicacies are spread on a poisonous toadstool reinforces the message.

Dramatic Entrance

The popularity of the mushroom as a faery seat extended to nineteenth-century stage productions of A Midsummer Night's Dream. *The actress Ellen Terry made her debut, aged eight, as Puck in a popular production of the play. She made her entrance by dramatically rising through the floor on a mushroom, but one night caught and broke her toe in the stage machinery. A true professional, she carried on regardless and, suitably impressed, the director Charles Kean, doubled her salary for her heroic performance.*

21

The FAERY RING

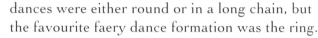

The faeries of folk legend rarely worked. Most of their time was spent dancing, and there are countless references to their love of music and delight in dancing.

Sometimes human musicians were lured into faeryland to accompany their faery dances. Occasionally the faeries were able to bestow the gift of music on selected mortals. Legend has it that an untalented and despised member of the celebrated McCrimmon family of Scottish musicians was transformed into a famous piper after meeting a little faery man. Many faery tunes are supposed to have been learned by mortal pipers. The reel tune *The Faery Dance* is one, while the popular tune *The Londonderry Air* is believed to be of faery origin, because no human words seem to fit it.

The faery time, of course, is night. Descriptions abound in folklore collections of elfin revellers dancing away in the moonlight to the sound of the harp or pipes. The earliest dances were either round or in a long chain, but the favourite faery dance formation was the ring.

Round dances originated from fertility rites and the faery ring is an echo of popular country customs, such as dancing around the maypole. The faeries are constantly found with one or other of the basic male and female symbols. The phallic mushroom or toadstool around which the faeries of later folklore are popularly believed to have danced is an obvious example.

A faery ring was the name generally given to circles of withered or bright green grass, around which elves would nightly cavort. Scientific explanations for the phenomenon have been proposed, but Devonshire folk legend fancied they were caused by elves 'catching colts found in the fields and riding them round and round'.

The seventeenth-century antiquarian John Aubrey reported that a curate, Mr Hart, had come across a faery ring in progress one evening while walking on the Wiltshire Downs. He was 'very greatly amaz'd' and was unable to run away, because he was kept there 'in a kind of enchantment'. The faeries were like 'pigmies or very small people, dancing rounde and rounde, and singing and making all manner of small, odd noyses'.

Water for elf, not water for self • You've lost your right eye, your child and yourself •

I have never seen a man faery or a woman faery, but my mother saw a troop of them. She herself and other maidens of the townland were milking cows in the evening gloaming, when they observed a flock of fairies reeling and setting upon the green plain in front of the knoll…Bell-helmets of blue silk covered their heads, and garments of green satin covered their bodies, and sandals of yellow membranes covered their feet. Their heavy brown hair was streaming down their waist, and its lustre was of the fair golden sun of summer. Their skin was as white as the swan of the wave, and their voice was as melodious as the mavis of the wood, and they themselves were as beauteous of feature and as lithe of form as a picture, while their step was as light and stately and their minds as sportive as the little red hind of the hill.

FROM AN 1877 COLLECTION OF SCOTTISH FOLK STORIES.

WISHING WELLS

THE CELTS believed that springs and wells were the entrances to the mysterious Underworld. Similar beliefs exist in folk legend, and enchanted springs and wells were seen as the entrance to faeryland. Their magic waters, or their resident faeries, were thought to be able to cure illness or to bestow good luck.

Writing in the seventeenth century, John Fletcher described a magic well with miraculous powers in *The Faithful Shepherdess*:

A vertuous well, about whose flowry banke
The nimble-footed Fairies dance their rounds,
By the pale moon-shine, dipping oftentimes
Their stolen Children, so to make them free
From dying flesh and dull mortalitie.

A Northumberland tale tells of how a crippled knight who was suffering from leprosy, and had lost his hands and feet to the disease, crawled into the Bubbling Well. When he climbed out he had not only been cured of his leprosy, but had recovered his hands and feet. An evil warlock tried to pollute the well by throwing a bad old witch into it, but the water rose up and poured down the hill, taking her body with it. The water carried on rising and eventually washed both the warlock and the witch out to sea.

At the Loch Siant Well on the island of Skye, people in need of a cure for their illnesses had to walk three times round the spring after drinking its water. At Fivepennies Well on the Hebridean island of Eigg, the water was said to cure the first disease of anyone who drank it, but if a stranger lay beside the well at night time, he would contract some bodily deformity.

The faery guardians of magic water manifested themselves in a variety of shapes. At a well near Banff in Scotland, the resident spirit appeared as a fly. If it was lively, it was a good omen. If it was listless, bad luck was sure to follow. The faery of Fiddlers Well, near Cromarty in Scotland, assumed the appearance of a bee. According to legend, the bee originally led William Fiddler to the well when he was ill, by calling him with the voice of a dead friend. He dug in the earth to find the spring, drank the water he found there, and was miraculously cured.

Offerings were made to the spirits of the wells. These could be garlands of flowers, rags tied to overhanging bushes, or pins or coins. Lovers would drop a pin into the water to see if their union was blessed by the resident spirit. If the pin floated, it was a good sign. If it sank, they knew it would be better to separate. In England, wells were traditionally dressed with garlands of flowers on Ascension Day, while in Ireland flowers were offered at the traditional festival of dead kinsfolk on the first day of August.

On the Devil's Causeway in Shropshire, the Devil and his imps were believed to preside over a well in the shape of frogs. The folk tradition of devilish frogs lurking in deep waters was transformed into faery stories.

In *The Frog Prince*, a princess promises to marry a speaking frog she meets by a spring of water in a wood, if it will return her golden ball to her. The ball is returned but she refuses to keep her promise. She is persecuted by the creature until she agrees to let him into her bed. The frog then transforms himself into a handsome prince. 'He told her that he had been enchanted by a malicious fairy, who had changed him into the form of a frog, in which he was fated to remain till some princess should take him out of the spring and let him sleep in her bed for three nights.'

IN their ELEMENT

FAERY SPIRITS of the air, were mentioned as the supreme shape shifters by Henry More in *The Prae-Existency of the Soul*:

> But those of air can easily convert
> Into new forms, and then again revert,
> One while a man, after a comley maid,
> And then all suddenly to make thee stert,
> Like leaping Leopard he'll thee invade.

John Milton shared the same view in *Paradise Lost*:

> For Spirits when they please
> Can either Sex assume, or both
> In what shape they choose
> Dilated or condens't, bright or obscure,
> Can execute their aerie purposes.

The most celebrated airy faery is the aptly named Ariel, from Shakespeare's *The Tempest*. A far cry from the earthy hobgoblin Puck, Ariel is a predominantly invisible being that 'drinks the air before him'. At the end of the play, when Ariel is freed it is into the air, Prospero tells him:

> Then to the elements
> Be free, and fare thou well.

The seventeenth-century faery authority Robert Kirk described the bodies of the faeries as being made of congealed air, rather like Ariel. In *The Secret Commonwealth of Elves, Fauns and Fairies*, he wrote: 'These Siths or Fairies…are said to be of a middle Nature betwixt Man and Angel, as were Daemons thought to be of old; of intelligent studious Spirits and light changeable Bodies (lyke those called Astral), somewhat of the Nature of a condensed Cloud and best seen in Twilight. These Bodies be so plyable thorough the Subtilty of the Spirits that agitate them, that they can make them appear or disappear at Pleasure.'

While Ariel and his ilk were manifestations of etherealized faeries and were as light and insubstantial as air, mermaids were altogether more substantial. Voluptuous sea nymphs, they were faery manifestations, symbolic of the shifting dual nature of the sea as both life giver and destroyer.

There were freshwater faery sirens too. Like the mermaids, they were avid for human life. The River Ribble, in northern England, was regarded as the haunt of a sinister spirit called Peg O'Nell, who probably derived from a Roman goddess. She required an animal sacrifice every seven years. If this was not forthcoming, she demanded a human victim instead. The Shellycoat was a male water spirit that frequented Scottish streams. Like the Willo'-the-wisp, he delighted in leading travellers astray.

Mermaids

In enchanted underwater worlds, individual faery spirits might be encountered. Best known are the mermaids, the alluring sirens of the sea with women's bodies and faces, but monstrous fishy tails. Inland variants include Lorelei, the German siren from the River Rhine. The English water demon Peg Powler, who haunted the River Tees, was said to entice her victims to a watery death and then devour them. Local people called the dense froth on the river 'Peg Powler's suds' and the scattered foam 'Peg Powler's cream'.

SMALLER and SMALLER

THE MINIATURE nature faery popularized by Shakespeare and the Jacobean poets has become a favourite image, but the faeries of folk legend came in a variety of sizes and also had the power to appear larger or smaller by changing their shape.

As the Irish poet W. B. Yeats commented 'Do not think the faeries are always little. Everything is capricious about them, even their size. They seem to take what size or shape pleases them…faeries in Ireland are sometimes as big as we are, sometimes bigger, and sometimes, as I have been told, about three feet high.'

The faeries of medieval romances, the knights and enchantresses, were generally of human or more than human size. In the fourteenth-century English poem *Sir Gawain and the Green Knight*, the faery knight and his enchantress wife are human sized and because of this Sir Gawain does not suspect their faery nature at first. He learns subsequently, unfortunately, that his genial host is actually the Green Knight and that his wife is Morgan le Fay.

The faery ladies encountered by Wild Edric in an English folk legend collected by Walter Map in the twelfth century were described as taller and larger than women of the human race.

Faeries of mortal height featured in ancient Scottish ballads appear to have had human dimensions. The courtly Irish faery people, the Tuatha de Danaan, were also generally described as resembling mortals.

There are no fixed rules in faeryland, however, and smaller faeries also feature in the early descriptions. Scottish ballads included shorter beings, such as *The Wee Wee Man*:

> His legs were scant a shathmont's length
> [six inches]
> And thick and thimber was his thie;
> Atween his brows there was a span,
> And atween his shoulders there was three.

The faeries had the power to change their appearance at will, as in the tale 'Cherry of Zennor', included in Robert Hunt's *Popular Romances of the West of England* (1865). A young Cornish girl was hired as a nanny by a mortal-sized faery, 'a well-dressed gentleman', whom she met on her way to a local fair. They worked together in his beautiful garden 'where flowers of all seasons grew and flowered together', and he gave her a kiss at the end of every row. When she broke her promise to him, however, and anointed her own eye with magic ointment, she saw her faery lover in quite a different light: 'she saw

28

numbers of tiny people dancing, and to her fury
she saw her master among them, as tiny
as they were, and on very familiar terms
with the little faery ladies.'

Shape-shifting gave the faeries the power to be
bigger but, according to the Cornish tale 'The
Faery Dwelling on Selena Moor', the act of
changing shape itself made them get smaller and
smaller, until they reached the size of an ant,
then wilted into nothingness.

LARGER than LIFE

THE DENIZENS of faeryland might manifest themselves in humanoid or monstrous forms – and the monsters that were spawned by folk mythology were truly terrifying. The giants and dragons of early legend were always larger than life and endowed with superhuman strength and colossal appetites.

The earliest giants of legend were usually cannibals and often rapists, and tales of cannibalistic giants continued in faery mythology. In stories about Red Etin, the Scottish monster 'with the thre heydis', he would shout:

> Snouk but and snouk ben,
> I find the smell of an earthly man;
> Be he living, or be he dead,
> His heart this night shall kitchen my bread.

The giant's traditional cry of 'Fee, fi, fo, fum', from popular faery stories such as *Jack the Giantkiller*, was a variant of Red Etin's threats, although Jack's giant favoured grinding up human bones to make his bread.

In later tradition, giants were conquered by subtlety rather than force. They were still enormously strong but they had become stupid. Some were cowardly as well, notably the Giant Gorm, who created Maes Knoll in the valley of the River Avon when he carelessly dropped a giant-sized shovel of earth, and Wansdyke. When he was confronted by an angry Lord of Avon, however, he ran away, tumbled over his own toes and fell straight into the Bristol Channel.

Effigies of giants were used, historically, to frighten the enemy away or to slow them down by magic. Sometimes images of giants were cut into the turf. A well known example is the Cerne Giant, a colossal figure, wielding a club, cut into the chalk on a hill near Cerne Abbas in Dorset, England. He is believed to be the outline of a giant killed by the local people as he slept, after feasting on their cattle.

The Foolish Giant

The giants of later tradition might not have been as horrific as their forbears but they could be horrifyingly stupid. The Cornish giant Carn Galva is a dramatic example. Carn Galva was a kindly ogre but frighteningly unaware of his own strength, as is revealed in Traditions and Hearthside Stories of West Cornwall *by William Bottrell. The book tells of how Carn Galva's best friend was a mere mortal. When the two parted one day, however, the foolish ogre*

THE GIANT'S SHADOW

made a careless mistake with fatal consequences. He 'tapped his playfellow on the head with the tips of his fingers. At the same time he said "Be sure to come again tomorrow, my son, and we will have a capital game of bob". Before the word "bob" was swell out of the giant's mouth, the young man dropped at his feet – the giant's fingers had gone right through his playmate's skull.' Horrified by what he had done, Carn Galva went into a decline and, seven years later, died of a broken heart.

TRANSPORTS *of* DELIGHT

MOST PEOPLE, if asked to describe a faery would begin with the wings. Curiously, they are a relatively recent development. The winged faery made its first appearance in Alexander Pope's 18th-century poem *The Rape of the Lock*. The rise of the winged faery owed much

to the influence of classical art. The Greek goddess of the soul, Psyche, was often shown as a miniature human being with butterfly wings. Renaissance artists enjoyed painting the legend of Cupid and frequently provided him with faery-like female attendants with butterfly

wings. The small winged cupids of Greek and Roman sculpture also influenced later writers and artists to invest their faeries with decorative wings to make them more ornamental.

Another source of inspiration was the Bible and its descriptions of angels with feathered wings. Faeries have been depicted on occasion with feathered wings, like angels, and the Christmas tree faery probably derives from an angel. Indeed, the faeries were commonly believed to be fallen angels.

Shakespeare's faeries were small enough to ride on the back of a bird, or a bat, as Ariel did in *The Tempest*, while Queen Mab in *Romeo and Juliet* is drawn through the air by 'a team of little atomies' by a waggoner who was a 'small grey-coated gnat'. His descriptions of the minute decorative pleasures inspired later faery poets to go into even greater ornamental detail in their description of the faery world. The close association of faeries and insects gave rise not just to the winged faery but to yet more imaginative descriptions in literature and art of ways in which they were transported through the skies.

Some to the Sun, their Insect-Wings unfold,
Waft on the Breeze, or sink in Clouds of Gold,
Transparent Forms, too fine for mortal Sight,
Their fluid Bodies half dissolv'd in Light.

FLIGHTS of FANCY

THE FAERIES of folk legend used magic spells to levitate themselves and fly about their business. The idea of faeries having wings themselves was a much later concept.

Traditionally, the faeries hopped aboard transformed ragwort stems or bundles of grasses, using them like a witch's broomstick. They had to utter the magic password, however, to get airborne.

The bold Scottish Laird of Duffus used a levitation spell on himself in a flight with very embarrassing personal consequences, according to Sir Walter Scott in his *Minstrelsy of the Scottish Border*. On uttering the magic password, 'he immediately found himself whirled away in the air with a troop of faeries to the King of France's cellar. There they caroused all night so merrily that the Laird fell asleep and was left behind. The royal butler found him next day, still asleep with a cup of curious workmanship in his hand.' Fearing the worst, the laird was taken to the king. Fortunately for him, the king believed his extraordinary explanation for drinking the night away in the royal wine cellar and generously sent him back home with the faery cup.

Donning a white faery cap was another traditional aid to levitation. In E. M. Leather's *The Folk-Lore of Herefordshire*, a boy who got lost in a wood, woke up at midnight to see the faeries leaping out of bed, putting on little white caps and then appearing to fly away. The boy seized a white cap, and was immediately transported to the faery ring outside the door of a hut where the little women were dancing.

The boy flew with the faeries to a gentleman's house, where he disgraced himself by drinking

In the hinder end of Harvest, on ahallow even,
Quhen our good neighboures doth ryd, if I reid rycht,
Sum buckled on a buinvand, and some one a bene,
Ay trottand in trowpse from the twylychte;
Some saidland a sho aipe all graithid into greine,
Some hobland one and ane hempstalk, hovand to the heicht.
The King of pharie, and his Court, with the elph queine,
With mony elrich Incubus was rydand that nycht.

too much wine and falling asleep, rather than flying back home with his faery companions. The angry gentleman wanted the boy to be hanged as a thief for helping himself to his wine. Things looked grim but at the eleventh hour, when the boy was standing on the scaffold, a faery intervened to save him. She put a magic white cap on his head and he flew away to safety.

Do you seek the road to Fairyland
    I'll tell, it's easy, quite
Wait till a yellow moon gets up
    O'er purple seas by night,
And gilds a shining pathway
    That is sparkling diamond bright
Then, if no evil power be nigh
    To thwart you, out of spite,
And if you know the very words
    To cast a spell of might,
You get upon a thistledown,
    And, if the breeze is right,
You sail away to Fairyland
    Along this track of light.

ERNEST THOMPSON SETON, *THE ROAD TO FAIRYLAND*

BEASTLY ENCHANTMENTS

THE FAERIES were reputed to have their own domestic animals, just as mortals do. Indeed, some animals were regarded as members of the faery race.

Cats were popularly believed to be evil faeries, although Lady Wilde in *Ancient Legends, Mystic Charms and Superstitions of Ireland*, published in 1887, recounts a story about a friendlier faery cat: an old woman was sitting up late, spinning, when there came several knocks at her cottage door. She let in a black cat, and two white kittens, who made themselves comfortable by the fire. But the black cat told her to stop spinning and go to bed, because she had stopped the faeries from coming in and enjoying themselves. 'And if it hadn't been for myself and my daughters, it's dead you'd be now, the cat said,' explaining that she had been spared because of her kindness to her three feline visitors.

There were faery dogs too. Unlike the demon dogs, such as the Mauthe Doog, which were faeries in their own right, these were enchanted animals who were generally white, rather than black, and often had red ears. A couple of red-eared faery dogs in Somerset were described as being bigger than Irish wolfhounds, although very similar in appearance. Faery hounds were spotted on the Isle of Man: 'The little white faery dog with something red about his head heralded the approach of his owners, especially when they wanted to come indoors for shelter on a cold winter night,' W. W. Gill wrote in *A Second Manx Scrapbook*.

Faery horses were beautiful creatures. Once again, however, it was their distinctive colour that distinguished them from other horses. In the ballad *Young Tamlane*, Jenny was able to rescue the mortal hero from the faeries, because only he rode a 'milk-white steed'. When explaining how to carry out the rescue, when the faeries were out riding, Tamlane said:

> O first let pass the black, lady,
> And syne let pass the brown,
> But quickly run to the milk-white steed,
> Pu ye his rider down.

Faery enchantment could transform a mortal into animal form, of course. In *A Midsummer Night's Dream*, the weaver Bottom is memorably transformed by Puck into an ass. 'O Monstrous! O strange! We are haunted. Pray, masters! Fly, masters! Help!' exclaim his terrified companions, when he appears with the head of a donkey.

A handsome prince who has been turned into a loathsome animal is a recurrent theme in faery stories. In *Beauty and the Beast*, Beauty's initial fear and disgust towards the Beast turns to love as she gets to know him, and eventually she tells the Beast that she cannot live without him.

ENTER the KING

THE BEST KNOWN faery king is Oberon. Shakespeare was following an established tradition in naming his faery king Oberon in *A Midsummer Night's Dream*, although Auberon or Oberycom were popular names in early Renaissance times.

Oberon was the faery king in the fifteenth-century French prose romance *Huon of Bordeaux*, which was translated into English in 1548 by Lord Berners. For the first time in a romance, the faery king was miniaturized. Oberon was described as being the size of a three year-old child, as the result of a curse laid on him by a malicious faery at his christening. In the tale, Oberon is initially feared as a fiend, but turns out to be a friendly and virtuous ruler.

By miniaturizing Oberon in *A Midsummer Night's Dream*, Shakespeare was continuing the concept of a diminutive faery king. His faery sovereign is represented as a powerful but essentially kindly spirit. He intervenes to set the lovers' affairs to rights in the play and goes with Titania to bless Theseus's marriage bed. Unlike his more fearsome folk ancestors, he is not a

creature of the night. He prefers to leave before sunrise but he boasts his power of outstaying the sun. The first cock crow was traditionally the signal for a massed faery exit.

His faeryland caught the imagination of a group of British sixteenth-century poets and a cult of the miniature sprang up. One of the most famous faery poems of the period was *Nimphidia, the Court of Fayrie*, by Michael Drayton. He called his faery king Oberon but chose Mab, not Titania, as the name for his faery queen.

Unlike Shakespeare's more powerful sovereign, Drayton's Oberon is a victim of magic, rather than its master. A far less dignified creation, he is dramatically scaled down and because he cannot fly, is forced to travel around on the backs of insects.

In *Oberon's Diet* by Robert Herrick, the reader is treated to a fanciful description of the varied delicacies on which a diminutive faery king might dine:

> The hornes of paperie Butterflies,
> Of which he eates, and tastes a little
> Of that we call the Cuckoes spittle.

Pleasantly gorged, the tiny monarch proceeds to join Queen Mab in the bedchamber, in Herrick's equally elaborate poem *Oberon's Palace*. It is hung with snake skins and the eyes from peacocks' tails and lit by glow worms' eyes and the reflections from fish scales.

King Oberon was depicted as a miniature Apollo in most Victorian faery paintings, but on stage, the character was most commonly acted by a woman. The prevailing theory was that a female was by nature more likely to be convincingly ethereal.

Attitudes to faeryland had changed by the beginning of the twentieth century. Oberon scarcely gets a mention in faery literature until the British writer Rudyard Kipling tells of earlier, darker beliefs in *Puck of Pook's Hill*, with its Oberon-like Sir Huon.

His belt was made of Mirtle leaves
Pleyted in small Curious theaves
Besett with Amber Cowslipp studdes
And fring'd a bout with daysie budds

In which his Bugle horne was hunge
Made of the Babling Echos tungue
Which sett unto his moone-burnt lippes
Hee windes, and then his fayries skipps.

FROM *OBERON'S APPARELL* BY SIR SIMEON STEWARD

With this field-dew consecrate,
Every fairy takes his gait,
And each several chamber bless,
Through this palace, with sweet peace;
Ever shall in safety rest,
And the owner of it blest.
   Trip away;
   Make no stay;
Meet me all by break of day.

FROM OBERON'S FINAL SPEECH,
A MIDSUMMER NIGHT'S DREAM

Her shirt was o' the grass-green silk,
Her mantle o' the velvet fyne,
At ilka tett of her horse's mane,
Hung fifty siller bells and nine.

The COURTLY QUEEN

IN THE beginning, faery stories were circulated by word of mouth. Many of the earliest have been passed down through ballads. One early ballad, *Thomas the Rhymer*, tells how the Queen of Elfland fell in love with Thomas and carried him off to her faery kingdom, where he remained for seven years. The Queen of Elfland is described as a beautiful, imperious faery monarch.

In the Scottish ballad *Young Tam Lin*, the faery queen is followed by three separate courts when she went out night riding, the 'head court' being clad in robes of green and composed of knights and ladies.

There is a long tradition of faery kings and queens in Irish legend. The Daoine Sidhe, the faery people of Ireland, were generally supposed to be the descendants of gods and goddesses of earlier belief. They had their own courts and enjoyed all the aristocratic pursuits of medieval chivalry, such as hunting, riding, music and dancing. Powerful Irish faery queens included Queen Onagh, reputed to rule all of faery Ireland with the assistance of Cleena, a tributary queen of Munster, and her two sub-queens, Queen Evin of North Munster and Queen Ainé of South Munster.

The concept of an alluring, courtly faery queen, similar to such powerful sovereigns, has persisted in the popular imagination, alongside that of a coarser country queen, based on folk beliefs. The most potent evocation of a rarefied faery sovereign is Titania in Shakespeare's *A Midsummer Night's Dream*, who is described as a kind of mythological goddess. The triple goddess Diana was believed to be an enchantress in her third manifestation as Hecate, because she had already been associated with the faeries in folk tradition.

In Edmund Spenser's allegorical romance *The Faerie Queene*, Queen Elizabeth I was Gloriana, the Faery Queene. Despite the name, there are no obvious links with faeryland but many believe that Shakespeare too modelled his faery queen Titania on Queen Elizabeth. The image of Elizabeth as a Queen-Moon was much used by contemporary poets. Diana was also regarded as a moon goddess, which lends additional credence to the Titania-Elizabeth association.

Significantly, Shakespeare chose a name not commonly used for the faery queen, and one with closer links to classical mythology. He appears to have been influenced by the Roman poet Ovid's *Metamorphoses*, and there are certainly many references to that work in his play: Ovid's retelling of the story features the goddess Diana, who is also called Titania, there is a wooded grove and attendant nymphs, while Actaeon metamorphoses into a stag.

In their pictorial interpretations of *A Midsummer Night's Dream*, artists such as Henry Fuseli and Sir Joseph Noel Paton surrounded their faery sovereigns with attendants. While Fuseli's faery court and imperious queen harks back to more fearsome nature spirits, however, the later paintings of Paton show a more decorative and whimsical host of attendants for a more passive faery queen.

Queen of the Nursery

As the nineteenth century progressed, the popular image of the faery king and queen became increasingly sentimental. Our modern day notion of elves as boys and faeries as girls was shaped largely by the popular Victorian artist Richard 'Dicky' Doyle, who introduced an element of childish love and behaviour into his faery paintings.

A POCKET VENUS

THE IMAGE of a siren-like faery enchantress is well established and has provided the inspiration for countless early ballads and stories. In the fourteenth-century English poem *Sir Gawain and the Green Knight*, a beautiful faery seductress, Morgan le Fay, comes to Gawain in bed and tries to persuade him to make love to her.

> In thin array after a pleasant guise
> When her loose gown from her shoulders
>   did fall,
> And she caught me in her arms long and small
> Therewithal sweetly did me kiss
> And softly said, 'Dear heart, how like you this?'
> It was no dream; I lay broad waking.

Victorian prudery made nudity in art, in general terms, a dangerous subject. The high esteem in which classical art was held, however, meant that, paradoxically, it was almost de rigueur to portray nudes in scenes of classical myth. This contradictory attitude persisted in some quarters until the end of the nineteenth century.

Henry Fuseli was one of the first artists to recognize the enormous visual potential of folk superstition. His late eighteenth-century paintings inspired by *A Midsummer Night's Dream* portray Titania as a voluptuous Venus and Oberon as her Apollo. Changes in attitudes towards women is reflected in the evolving image of Titania during the Victorian age. A process of super-refinement of feminine innocence was apparent; any malevolent tendencies were increasingly channelled into the goblin entourage, which represented the male principle.

As the century progressed, a reaction set in against Fuseli's faery viragos, who clearly wielded the wand in faeryland. Richard and Samuel Redgrave, the authors of *A Century of Painters of the English School*, wrote that they found Fuseli's women 'somewhat more than masculine...absolutely coarse and at times disgusting'.

Successive faery painters elaborated on the concept of the faery queen as a contemporary Venus to a point where, suffused with an unearthly radiance as in the paintings of Sir Joseph Noel Paton, Richard Dadd and John Simmons, she took on an almost sacrosanct quality. The idea of the faery queen as a madonna-like figure appears in Dadd's *Come unto these Yellow Sands*, where she and her attendants are shown as a religious group watching over the faery dance from an arched rock.

The concept is echoed in Paton's faery paintings, but this time with a greater emphasis on the erotic. His Titanias assume the appearance of sexual madonnas, an interesting development in the light of the artist's later conversion to religious themes.

The ingenuousness of the faery trappings served as a foil for discreet eroticism. The curious combination of the worldly and unworldly received fascinating expression in Simmons' series of paintings in the 1860s and 1870s, which were devoted to Titania, and display both a childlike naiveté and a fully adult appreciation of feminine physical charms.

Clad in a wisp of transparent gauze, Simmons' curvaceous faery queen drifts through the landscape in a narcissistic daydream. A more passive concept of womanhood found a bizarre reflection in the concept of the tiny, immobilized faery odalisque. This was a favourite theme and one often treated in an overtly erotic way, as in the many scenes depicting the sleeping Titania surrounded by voyeurs in the form of the armoured Oberon and his faery warriors. Such mixtures of ingenuousness and a calculated eroticism created an uneasy sexual ambiguity which frequently borders on the discreetly pornographic.

Out of this wood do not desire to go:
Thou shalt remain here, whe'r thou wilt or no.
I am a spirit of no common rate;
The summer still doth tend upon my state;
And I do love thee: therefore, go with me;
I'll give thee fairies to attend on thee,
And they shall fetch thee jewels from the deep,
And sing, while thou on pressed flowers dost sleep:
And I will purge thy mortal grossness so
That thou shalt like an airy spirit go.

WILLIAM SHAKESPEARE, *A MIDSUMMER NIGHT'S DREAM*

A COUNTRY QUEEN

If ye will with *Mab* find grace,
Set each Platter in his place;
Rake the Fier up, and get
Water in, ere Sun be set.
Wash your Pailes, and clense your Dairies;
Sluts are loathsome to the Fairies:
Sweep your house: Who doth not so,
Mab will pinch her by the toe.

ROBERT HERRICK, *THE HESPERIDES*

QUEEN MAB was the most popular
choice of faery queen in sixteenth-
and seventeenth-century literature.
She was a far less dignified sovereign than
the courtly Queen Titania of Shakespeare's
A Midsummer Night's Dream, and was drawn
more directly from country superstitions.

Some folklorists believe Mab derived from
Habundia, a witch-like faery goddess of the
medieval period. Habundia was a maternal
spirit and feasts were spread out for her in
houses she was believed to frequent, just as
food was left for the ancient French fatae,
the faeries who presided over childbirth.

The name was possibly a variant of maban,
the Welsh word for baby, a further maternal
association, which would help to explain
Mab's close connection with childbirth in folk
belief. In *Romeo and Juliet*, Shakespeare
describes her as 'the faeries' midwife', and

when he wrote the play she was a well known faery in his native Warwickshire. Instead of describing mortals led astray by the faeries as 'pixy-led', people in that county called them 'Mab-led'.

Mab is believed by some experts to derive from the warlike Queen Maeve of Ireland. Maeve was popularly believed to be queen of the Irish faeries. In one ancient tale she is described as 'Maeve the Sidhe-Queen'. Mab might have been regarded as a faery queen because of her links with Maeve. Alternatively, the use of 'queen' might simply mean 'female', from the old English word 'quen', meaning female.

The Queen Mab pictured in *Romeo and Juliet* is very different from Shakespeare's Titania, but she continues the miniaturization process. However, she still has the capacity to strike fear into the hearts of men, in true faery style. Like the faery 'night-mare', she is a bringer of troubled dreams when she 'gallops night by night'. In her role as faery midwife, Shakespeare's Mab is a figure of fear as well. She is the:

Hag, when maids lie on their backs,
That presses them and learns them first to bear.

The dramatist Ben Jonson, in his *Entertainment at Althorpe*, described Mab as a similar faery to Shakespeare's Puck. She is:

…the mistris-Faerie,
That doth nightly rob the dayrie;
And can hurt, or help the cherning,
(As she please) without discerning.

In the Jacobean poet Michael Drayton's *Nimphidia*, Mab is faery queen and married to Oberon, but they are essentially comic creations of insect-like proportions. In their minuscule faeryland, a cowslip bell is not the refuge of an individual faery but a hall or faery court for Queen Mab.

The faery folk tradition was treated most fully by the poet John Milton in his description of country people's story-telling in *L'Allegro*. Here he records local tales of 'How Faery Mab the junkets eat', linking her with the domestic hobgoblins who were thought to keep an eye on the home, but who were easily offended.

HOBGOBLINS and BROWNIES

THERE ARE many folk tales that tell of faeries helping, or hindering, around the house. The best known domestic spirit was called a Brownie in Scotland and much of England, a Bwca in Wales and a Pixie in the West Country. Puck and Robin Goodfellow are well-known faeries of the Brownie-type, and there are many more bearing different names, according to the part of the country from which they come.

The concept of a faery connected with the hearth and home has links with far earlier beliefs. The Ancient Romans worshipped household gods, whose duties were to protect the home and ward off dangers, and on special family occasions offerings of food and wine were made to them in order to please them.

The character of the Brownie is very similar. It was popularly believed that he made himself responsible for the house in which he lived and that he would come out at night to finish any jobs that still needed doing. Unlike the Roman household gods, however, a Brownie was not bound to a particular place. He was also more fickle with his favours. A Brownie might easily move away if a household displeased him. Many stories turn on the touchy nature of the Brownie and the fear that, if crossed, he might do something really nasty.

According to legend, most Scottish families had a household Brownie. 'About forty or fifty years ago,' wrote the chronicler John Brand in 1703, 'almost every family had a "browny" or evil spirit so-called which served them, to whom they gave a sacrifice for his services.'

Among the more notable Brownies in service to Scotland's greatest families was the faery known simply as 'the little one' attached to the MacKays of Kintyre. He followed the chief of the clan throughout the Peninsular War, warding off any French bullets that came his master's way. The resident Brownie at the Doune of Rothiemurchus fared less well with his chieftain, however. According to Sir Walter Scott in his *Minstrelsy of the Scottish Border*, he was driven away because the master of the house was unable to stand the noise his faery helper made when scouring the pots and pans.

The earlier Brownies were as tall as humans or taller, but they diminished in size, as belief in them declined. They were exceptionally strong – one was reputed to thresh as much corn in one night as twenty lusty men – and fearsome to look at. The name apparently derived from the matted brown hair that was commonly believed to cover most of their body. A Brownie's feet and hands sometimes had no separate toes or fingers, and might have long curved claws.

Offerings of food and drink were traditionally left out at night to keep a resident Brownie sweet. Describing the custom in *Folk-Lore of the Northern Counties*, William Henderson wrote: 'He is allowed his little treats, however, and the chief of these are knuckled cakes made of meal warm from the mill, toasted over the embers and spread with honey.' In parts of Scotland milk fresh from the cow was poured into hollow 'Browney's stones'.

The best known Brownie in England in the sixteenth and seventeenth centuries was Robin Goodfellow. His night-time labours frequently had a sexual connotation in contemporary literature. Shakespeare's Puck is also referred to as Robin Goodfellow in *A Midsummer Night's Dream*, and his domestic chores were metaphors for the sex act. 'Are not you he', enquires a faery in the play, 'That…bootless makes the breathless housewife churn'. The Brownie's phallic nature was emphasized by his nakedness. Traditionally, a gift of clothes would drive a Brownie away.

Hairy Meg

The Brownie was usually male, although there were exceptions. One of the more famous Brownies in Scottish tradition was Meg Mollach, reputedly attached to the Grants of Tullochgorm. She was married to 'Brownie Clod' and apparently derived her name from her luxurious head of hair.

Meg was believed to possess the gift of prophecy and the ability to change in shape. She served at table and would appear to be floating through the air, with whatever dish was requested. She cropped up in various different homes. In one farm, she agreed to help only if the servants were allowed to stay. When the farmer decided to dismiss his servants and rely on her, Meg tormented him until he agreed to re-employ them.

TRICKSTERS

WHILE the Brownie, or Hobgoblin, was generally believed to be a helpful faery that could turn nasty if it was annoyed, the Goblin and its variants were evil demons.

The Goblin became a general name for a type of frightening, dangerous spirit that delighted in tormenting mankind. Folk tradition divided the faeries into two separate orders, described as the 'Seelie Court' and the 'Unseelie Court'. Members of the 'Seelie Court' were well-disposed to mortals, but the faeries of the 'Unseelie Court' were imps from Hell.

The medieval Church condemned all faeries as devils. In *Malleus Maleficarum*, a fifteenth-century manual of witchcraft compiled by Heinrich Kramer and James Sprenger, who were two German Dominican Inquisitors, it was stated that 'the Good People as old women call them are witches, or devils in their forms'. Witchcraft trials were held in Scotland in the sixteenth and seventeenth centuries, in which dealings with faeries figure repeatedly as evidence of guilt.

One Scotswoman, Alison Peirson, who was tried in 1688, confessed to being visited by faeries who tormented her with a kind of paralysis. She claimed that her cousin had been carried away by the faeries but that he came back to warn her not to let herself get into their clutches, in case she might be used to pay the faery tribute to Hell.

A terrifying assault by such faery demons is powerfully described by the nineteenth-century poet Christina Rossetti in *Goblin Market*. By this time, evil faeries were popularly termed Goblins. Two sisters are tempted by the Goblins' forbidden fruit. One succumbs and almost dies. The other refuses them and manages to save her but is nearly killed in the attempt.

A Goblin variant, the Bogy or Bogey Best was one name for the Devil and an evil faery who was commonly used to frighten children into good behaviour. One example of the widespread practice, 'If tha doesna leave off shrikin', I'll fetch a black bogy to thee,' is given in *Rustic Speech and Folk-Lore* by E. M. Wright.

The 'Nursery bogies', as the folklorist Katharine Briggs described them in her *Dictionary of Fairies*, included a host of fearsome individuals, which included characters such as Mumpoker, Rawhead-and-bloody-bones, Tankerabogus, Tom Dockin, Tom-Poker, Churnmilk Peg and Awd Goggie.

The power to change shape made such goblins even more alarming. A ghostly headless Boggart was reputed to haunt the streets of Preston, in Lancashire. It rattled its chains as it walked but was finally exorcized in a nearby churchyard.

A Barguest in Yorkshire manifested itself as a headless man who disappeared in flames, a headless lady, a white cat, a rabbit and a black dog.

Red for Danger

Red is the colour of blood and some of the most evil Goblins were bloodthirsty fairies. The Scottish Redcap re-dyed his red cap in human blood. He was described by William Henderson in Folk-Lore of the Northern Counties, *published in 1879, as 'a short thickset old man, with long prominent teeth, skinny fingers armed with talons like eagles, large eyes of a fiery-red colour, grisly hair streaming down his shoulders, iron boots, a pikestaff in his left hand, and a red cap on his head'.*

Similar Goblins haunted lonely roads and led travellers astray. A Brag in Lancashire followed a young man along the bank of the River Hodder. He could hear it howl but could see nothing. Suddenly, it manifested itself and its terrible eyes gleamed with supernatural fire. He struck it but his arm passed through its body. The encounter brought disaster on himself and his family. His wife and child died and he went mad.

Though the goblins cuffed and caught her,
Coaxed and fought her,
Bullied and besought her,
Scratched her, pinched her black as ink,
Kicked and knocked her,
Mauled and mocked her,
Lizzie uttered not a word;
Would not open lip from lip
Lest they cram a mouthful in.

CHRISTINA ROSSETTI, *GOBLIN MARKET*

SPINNERS and SHOEMAKERS

THE FAERIES had a great reputation for various skills. Faery women were famous as spinners and dyers, while the Leprechaun was a celebrated shoemaker.

Magical dyes were concocted from lichen, roots, bark, leaves and fruit. A faery pool near Loch Lomond in Scotland, where the water was of a peculiar shade of green, was believed to be the site of a faery dyeing factory. It was abandoned however, when their mortal neighbours came to investigate. The faeries did not have time to remove their equipment and were forced to leave it at the bottom of the pool – hence its strange colour.

The Scots had a faery patron of spinning called Habetrot. In 'The Three Spinners' by William Henderson in *Folk-Lore of the Northern Counties*, he describes how Habetrot helped a beautiful but lazy peasant girl to win the local laird for a husband by spinning for her.

The girl was ordered by her mother to spin, but could produce only 'a few feet of lumpy, uneven thread'. She came across an old woman, who was the skilled spinner Habetrot. She offered to spin the lint for the girl and promptly vanished. But the girl spied her in an underground faery hall: '…she saw a great cavern, with a number of queer old wives sitting spinning in it, each on a white marble stone.'

The local laird rode past the girl's cottage the following morning and was so impressed by the 'smoothness and evenness of the skeins' that the faeries had spun, that he proposed marriage to her on the spot. She accepted but knew there would be trouble, because he 'kept talking of all the fine yarn she would be spinning for him after the wedding'. She asked Habetrot for help, and she invited them both into her faery cavern. The laird asked why the spinners all had long lips and spoke with a stutter. When Habetrot told him that his new wife would be just like them soon, because she loved spinning so much, he lost all his enthusiasm for fine yarns and forbade her to do any more spinning.

Little Cowboy, what have you heard,
Up on the lonely rath's green mound?
Only the plaintive yellow bird
Sighing in sultry fields around,
Chary, chary, chary, chee-ee!-
Only the grasshopper and the bee?-
'Tip-tap, rip-rap,
Tick-a-tack-too!
Scarlet leather sewn together,
This will make a shoe.
Left, right, pull it tight;
Summer days are warm;
Underground in winter,
Laughing at the storm!'
Lay your ear close to the hill.
Do you not catch the tiny clamour,
Busy click of elfin hammer,
Voice of Leprecaun singing shrill
As he merrily plies his trade?

WILLIAM ALLINGHAM, *THE FAIRY SHOEMAKER*

Spinning Song

The fairies spinners who helped one lazy Scotswoman with her work, sang the following fairy chant:

Work, work, for little hand?
Can but little work command,
Some to tease and card and spin,
Some to oil and weave begin:
Some the water for waulking heat,
That we may her web complete.
Work, work, for a single hand
Can but little work command.

Some faeries preferred using man-made looms to their own and would steal into cottages at night to do their spinning. Residents of the Isle of Man tried to prevent them from doing this, but usually failed, as in the following story from Sophia Morrison's *Manx Fairy Tales*:

'Some time in the night my brother wakened me with a: "Shish! Listen boy, and look at the big light in the kitchen!"

"Listen!" I said, "it must be the Little Ones that's agate of the wheel!"

And both of us got very frightened. In the morning we told what we had seen.

"Aw, like enough, like enough," my Father said, looking at the wheel. "It seems your mother forgot to take the band off last night, a thing people should be careful about, for it's givin' Themselves power over the wheel."'

The Irish Leprechaun was generally described as a faery shoemaker. He commonly manifested himself as a little old man and was easily tracked down by the noise he made hammering.

FAERIES at PLAY

FAERYLAND is described as a place of endless delight, and legend has it that the faeries enjoyed the same sort of leisure activities as mortals.

The more aristocratic faeries, such as the Fays of medieval England, the Seelie Court of Scotland and the Daoine Sidh of Ireland, apparently favoured the courtly pursuits of dancing, music, hunting and processional rides.

The faeries often hunted faery deer. In *The Fairy-Faith in Celtic Countries*, W. Y. Evans Wentz recorded an eye-witness account of a faery hunt in progress near the mountain of Ben Bulbin: 'I knew a man who saw the Gentry hunting on the other side of the mountain. He saw hounds and horsemen cross the road and jump the hedge in front of him, and it was one o'clock at night. The next day he passed the place again, and looked for tracks of the huntsmen, but saw not a trace of tracks at all.'

Those faery hunters were mortal-sized, but as the descriptions of faeries became smaller and more ornamental in drama, poetry and literature, so their prey was radically reduced. Shakespeare's miniature faeries hunted bats and bumble bees.

By the nineteenth century, the fearsome faery hunters of folk legend were well and truly diminished. The 'elf-knight' in George Darley's poem *Sylvia: or, The May Queen* rides a grasshopper and is described thus:

His tough spear of a wild oat made,
His good sword of a grassy blade,
His buckram suit of shining laurel,
His shield of bark, emboss'd with coral.

Further popular faery sports included ball games, such as football and hurling. Chess was another favourite activity, and chess matches were sometimes used to defeat humans. The courtly Daoine Sidhe faeries of Ireland excelled at chess and were in the habit of challenging mortals to three games – the winner of each could choose his stake. In descriptions of these

matches, the human generally won the first two games and chose rich prizes, but the faery won the third and forced his luckless contestant to carry out some task that often proved fatal.

Such anti-social behaviour was a favourite faery activity and mischief making against mortals was a very popular pursuit. Shakespeare's Puck delights in making fools of humans, as he proudly relates in *A Midsummer Night's Dream*:

I am that merry wanderer of the night.
I jest to Oberon and make him smile,
When I a fat and bean-fed horse beguile,
Neighing in likeness of a filly foal:
And sometimes lurk I in a gossip's bowl,
In the very likeness of a roasted crab;
And, when she drinks against her lips I bob,
And on her withered dew-lap pour the ale.

FAERY MUSIC

FAERIES loved music and were skilled musicians. If they took a fancy to the music made by a mortal, however, they would whisk him or her off to faeryland to entertain them.

Sometimes the faeries acted more generously. Instead of taking human musicians captive, they bestowed even greater musical talents upon them. A famous family of Scottish pipers, the MacCrimmons, claimed they were given their musical talents by the faery gift of a black chanter to a younger son.

The lure of faery music was very powerful. Even saints could not resist it. In *The Fairy-Faith in Celtic Countries*, Evans Wentz records how St Patrick fared on hearing a faery concert. The saint was seated on a grassy knoll with an Irish king and his nobles, when a youth in a green cloak, carrying a kind of harp, appeared before them. The faery musician 'made for them music and minstrelsy, so that he sent them slumbering off to sleep. And the music was pleasing to Patrick, who said of it, "Good indeed it were, but for a twang of a fairy spell that infests it; barring which nothing could more nearly than it resemble Heaven's harmony."'

A skilful mortal musician could, on occasion, use that gift to rescue someone captured by the faeries. In the ancient Scottish ballad *King Orfeo*, the hero takes out his pipe to rescue his bride from faeryland. He plays it with such mastery that the faeries agree to let her go.

Fairies, arouse
Mix with your song
Harplet and pipe,
Thrilling and clear,
Swarm on the bows!
Chant in a throng!
Morning is ripe,
Waiting to hear.

WILLIAM ALLINGHAM,
A FOREST IN FAIRYLAND

A band of smugglers had a frightening
encounter with some faery musicians in *Stories
and Folk-Lore of West Cornwall* by William
Bottrell. They were snoozing on a beach one
summer's night when they were rudely
awakened by 'the shrill "tweeting" of "feapers"
[slit reeds]. Besides there was a constant
tinkling, just like old women make by rattling
pewter plates or brass pans to frighten swarming
bees home, or make them settle.'

The smugglers followed the sound and saw
'a score or so of little old-looking chaps; many
of them blew mouth-organs; some beat cymbals
or tambourines; whilst others played on jew's-
harps, or tweeted on May whistles and feathers.'
The faery musicians resented being watched,
however. They armed themselves with bows and
arrows, spears and slings and chased the
terrified smugglers off the beach and out to sea.

The FAERY DANCE

And about go wee,

Two by two and three by three

DANCING was a favourite pastime of the faeries, and references to faery dancers go back to the earliest written records.

The story of 'Wild Edric', related by Walter Map in the twelfth century, described the hero's first sight of his future wife, who was an elf maiden. She was dancing in a house in the forest of Clun. In a more

By the moone we sport and play,
With the night begins our day;
As we daunce, the deaw doth fall;
Trip it little urchins all,
Lightly as the little Bee,
Two by two and three by three:
And about go wee, and about go wee.

recent translation of the tale, Wild Edric saw 'a large company of noble ladies dancing. They were exceedingly beautiful, taller and larger than women of the human race, and dressed in gracefully-shaped linen garments. They circled round with smooth and easy motion, singing a soft low song of which the hunter could not understand the words. Among them was a maiden who excelled all the others in beauty, at the sight of whom our hero's heart was inflamed with love. Forgetting the fears of enchantment, which at the first moment had seized him, he hurried round the house, seeking an entrance, and having found it, he rushed in, and snatched the maiden who was the object of his passion

Round about, round about,
In a fair ring-a,
Thus we dance, thus we dance,
And thus we sing-a,
Trip and go, to and fro
Over this green-a,
All about, in and out,
For our brave Queen-a.

from her place in the moving circle. The dancers assailed him with teeth and nails, but backed by his page, he escaped at length from their hands, and succeeded in carrying off his fair captive.'

Folk legend and faery literature is full of references to dancing faeries. In the seventeenth century, a Cornish girl called Anne Jefferies created a sensation when she claimed she had been carried off to faeryland. Her description of the faery realm she entered has echoes of the courtly miniature faeryland imagined by Shakespeare, in which dancing was a central activity:

'She was surrounded by temples and palaces of gold and silver; there were trees covered with fruit and flowers, lakes full of golden and silver fish and bright-coloured birds singing all around. Hundreds of splendidly dressed people were walking in the gardens or dancing or sporting or reposing themselves in flowery arbours.'

Not all faery dancers were as elegant, however. The melancholy Trows of Shetland in Scotland enjoyed performing a very ungainly kind of dance. When they danced, the Trows were 'said to hop instead of walk, and to 'henk' when they danced. Their mode of dancing was very peculiar, they squatted till their knees were doubled up in front, and then they hopped about like pinioned fowls.'

A female Trow unable to find a dancing partner was forced to 'henk' on her own, according to a poignant ditty:

Hey! co Cuttie; an 'ho!' co Cuttie;
'An' wha'ill dance wi'me? co Cuttie.
Sho Luked aboot an' saw naebody;
Sae I'll henk awa mesel', co Cuttie.

FAERY FEASTS

country folk left a bowl of cream and a freshly baked cake out for their resident Brownie. In return, the faery would make himself useful around the house.

The Jacobean poet Robert Herrick described a fanciful miniature faery banquet in *Oberon's Feast*, which might also have pleased a vampire. It featured:

OPINIONS differed as to what the faeries ate, but it was generally agreed that they needed food. However, any mortal who tasted faery food would be whisked into faeryland and might never come back.

Robert Kirk, the seventeenth-century authority on faeries and author of *The Secret Commonwealth of Elves, Fauns and Fairies*, believed that different types of faeries required different kinds of nourishment. He remarked that the bodies of faeries were '...so spungious, thin and desecat, that they are fed only by sucking into some fine spiritous Liquors, that pierce like pure Air and Oyl; others feed more gross on the Foyson or substance of Corns and Liquors, or Corne it self that grows on the Surface of the Earth, which these Fairies steal away, partly invisible, partly preying on the Grain, as do Crowes and Mice; wherefore in this same Age, they are sometimes heard to bake Bread.'

Kirk explained that it was the Brownie faeries who had the heartiest appetites and enjoyed baking. This was a widespread belief and many

The broke-heart of a Nightingale
Ore-come in musicke; with a wine,
Ne're ravisht from the flattering Vine,
But gently prest from the soft side
Of the most sweet and dainty Bride,
Brought in a dainty daizie, which
He fully quaffs up to bewitch
His blood to height.

It was widely believed that the faeries extracted the vital essence of the plants on which they fed. According to Scottish legend, they feasted on the root of the silver weed, which was ploughed up in Spring. It was popularly known as 'the seventh bread' for that reason. They drank the milk of red deer, goats and cows, who they could milk themselves. A favourite time for faery meals taken in the Western Highlands was said to be when the sun was shining through the rain.

Lucky Escape

A seventeenth-century Cornish woman, Anne Jefferies, claimed that she was fed for six months by the elves with no ill effects. 'She forsook eating our victuals,' Moses Pitt wrote in an explanatory letter to the Bishop of Gloucester, 'and was fed by these fairies from that harvest time to the next Christmas-day.'

'Pluck not a hair!' a hidden rabbit cried,
'With but one hair he'll steal thy heart away,
Then only sorrow shall your lattice hide:
Go in! all honest pedlars come by day.'
There was dead silence in the drowsy wood;
'Here's syrup for to lull sweet maids to sleep;
And bells for dreams, and fairy wine and food
All day your heart in happiness to keep.'

WALTER DE LA MÀRE, *THE PEDLAR*

The FAERY RADE

WHEN the faeries went out riding at night, it was often in the form of a raiding party. Folklore is full of references to the their love of riding out in procession, and the fear the sight of such a cavalcade struck in mortal hearts, for if the faeries were out hunting their prey was likely to be mortal.

The concept of the faery 'rade' probably derived from an earlier belief in the 'Wild Hunt', a widely held superstition that stormy night winds were a manifestation of an aerial host sweeping by in hot pursuit of their quarry. It was thought that a faery cavalcade was actually a vision of the Host of the Dead.

The best faery steeds could gallop faster than the wind. According to Highland tradition, the wizard Michael Scot would use such a horse in an emergency. He first tried out a faery filly, but she was able to gallop only as fast as the wind. Eventually he found a horse that could travel at the speed of 'the thought of a maiden between two lovers'. When he arrived in Rome, the Pope was amazed to see that the wizard still had the snow of Scotland on his bonnet.

The horses ridden by the heroic faery people of Ireland, the Tuatha de Danann, who enjoyed the courtly pursuits of hunting and riding, were vividly described by Lady Wilde in *Ancient Legends, Mystic Charms and Superstitions of Ireland*:

'And the breed of horses they reared could not be surpassed in the world – fleet as the wind, with arched neck and broad chest and the quivering nostril, and the large eye that showed they were made of fire and flame. A splendid sight was the cavalcade of the Tuatha de Danaan knights. Seven-score steeds, each with a jewel on his forehead like a star, and seven-score horsemen, all the sons of kings, in their green mantles fringed with gold, and golden helmets on their head.'

The fairy steed ridden by Tam Lin in the ancient Scottish ballad is an echo of the Tuatha's fabled horses. He is:

...lighter than the wind;
Wi siller he is shod before,
Wi burning gowd behind.

Not all the faeries had the luxury of their own mounts. There are many folk references showing that faeries borrowed horses for their nightly

Caught in the Act

Watching a faery rade was considered a grave offence against the faeries, generally punishable by death. Most people sensibly avoided the routes favoured by the faeries for their nightly processions, although some Scottish peasants believed it was safe to watch as long as they used a faery repellent, such as pinning a branch of rowan over their cottage doors. It was believed that anyone inadvertently stumbling across a faery cavalcade would be taken away by the faeries and found dead the next day.

...lighter than the wind;
Wi siller he is shod before,
Wi burning gowd behind.

hunts and processions. The horses were returned in the morning covered in foam and quite exhausted, although they had apparently been in their stables all night. An angry horse owner on the Isle of Man claimed that he had lost three or four of his best horses, which had died as a result of their wild nocturnal ridings.

A Warwickshire tale concerns the fate of two Shetland ponies put out to grass near a wood haunted by the faeries. One morning they were discovered in a terrible state, having been bewitched by the faeries and they looked bad – quite different like'. Eventually they vanished and the real ponies, lame and over-ridden, were discovered later in the wood.

FAERY FUNERALS

THE CONCEPT of a faery dying seems to contradict the traditional belief that the faeries were death spirits. Nevertheless, there are references to faery mortality in folk legend.

The seventeenth-century authority on faeryland, Robert Kirk, certainly believed that faeries had a limited lifespan, like mortals. In *The Secret Commonwealth of Elves, Fauns and Fairies*, he wrote: 'They live much longer than wee; yet die at last or [at] least vanish from that State…they pass (after a long healthy Lyfe) into one Orb and Receptacle fitted for their Degree, till they come under the general Cognizance of the last Day.'

It was sometimes possible for a mortal to kill a faery. In the Scottish ballad of *Lady Isabel and the Elf-Knight*, the heroine charms her faery seducer into sleep and then stabs him to death. Similarly, the royal hero of the West Highland tale of *The Young King of Easaidh Ruadh* slays the Gruagach, a hairy goblin, with the sword of light that belonged to the faery's brother.

Estimates of the normal life span of a faery varied widely. In one Scottish legend, which tells of a faery who took the form of a man's kidnapped wife, it was just one year, because 'a faery can only live for twelve months in human form.'

Alternatively, a Welsh legend noted that the faeries lived seven years on the earth, seven years in the air and seven years underground.

The mourners were carrying flowering myrtle in their hands, and wearing wreaths of small roses. A little grave had been dug near the altar. The body was lowered into it, and the faeries threw their flowers after, crying aloud, "Our queen is dead!"' Then the faeries spotted him and rushed past him like a swarm of bees, 'piercing him with sharp points'.

The artist William Blake was fascinated by folk legend and painted several faery scenes. He also believed he had seen faeries and wrote an account of a faery funeral he had witnessed: 'I was walking alone in my garden, there was a great stillness among the branches and flowers & more than common sweetness in the air; I heard a low & pleasant sound & I know not whence it came. At last I saw the broad leaf of a flower move, & underneath I saw a procession of creatures the size & colour of green & grey grasshoppers, bearing a body laid out on a rose-leaf, which they buried with songs and disappeared.'

An old Gaelic rhyme

maintained that the faeries lived through nine ages 'with nine times nine periods of time in each':

Nine nines sucking the breast,
Nine nines unsteady, weak,
Nine nines footful, swift,
Nine nines able and strong.
Nine nines strapping, brown,
Nine nines victorious,
subduing,
Nine nines bonneted, drab,
Nine nines beardy, grey,
Nine nines on the
breasting beating
death
And worse to me these
miserable nine nines
Than all the other
short-lived nine
nines.

The funeral of a faery queen is described by Robert Hunt in *Popular Romances of the West of England*. It took place in a church, which is surprising, given the faeries' fear of God. An old Cornishman was returning home late at night, when he heard the bell of Lelant Church tolling and saw a lighted window. He peered in and saw 'a crowd of little people who were moving along the central aisle, with a bier carried between six of them. The body was uncovered; it was as small as the tiniest doll and of waxen beauty.

Titania makes sure that her donkey-headed lover does
not stray away by casting her own powerful magic spell:

Out of this wood do not desire to goe
Thou shalt remain here whether thou wilt or no.
I am a spirit of no common rate;
The summer still doth tend upon my state;
And I do love thee;
Therefore, go with me.

WILLIAM SHAKESPEARE, *A MIDSUMMER NIGHT'S DREAM*

MAGIC SPELLS

FOLK LEGEND is full of charms and spells that can be used to obtain power over faeries. Popular anti-faery tactics included crossing a stream to avoid faery pursuers, in the belief that running water was holy and could not be passed by evil spirits. Carrying a cross, particularly one made of iron, was also effective, as were bread and salt, which are both sacred symbols.

One way of avoiding the faeries in England was to turn your clothes inside out. 'I well remember,' says Denham in *The Denham Tracts*, edited by James Hardy, 'on more occasions than one, when a schoolboy, I have turned and worn my coat inside out in passing through a wood in order to avoid the good people.' The custom is also recalled in the ancient rhyme:

> Turn your clokes,
> For fairy folkes
> Are in old okes.

Several seventeenth-century magical manuscripts contain spells that can be used to either summon, dismiss or get help from the faeries. The following spell, dating from about 1600, is described as 'an excellent way to gett a Fayrie'. It advised that a glass measuring three inches in length and breadth should be placed for three Wednesdays and three Fridays in the blood of a white hen. The glass should then be washed in holy water and fumigated. Three-year-old hazel wands should then be peeled of their bark and the name of the faery who is to be summoned should be written three times on each stick. The sticks should be buried under a faery hill on a Wednesday and removed at either eight, three or ten o'clock. At the chosen hour, the faery can be called but only by someone in 'clean life' with their face turned towards the East. Once the faery appears, it must be bound to the prepared glass.

Three centuries on, a charm to make faeries visible is given in Claire Nahmad's *Fairy Spells*. The spell should be carried out in a garden with the help of a black cat, during an evening when the Northern Lights are in the sky. The cat should be stroked until she purrs contentedly. When she stretches for the first time, she should be anointed on the head with wine, making the sign of the cross, and the spellmaker should similarly anoint himself, or herself. The cat's tail should then be grasped and stroked swiftly three times over the person's left eye, then right eye, saying:

> Elves of the night, enchant my sight,
> Your forms for to see in moon or sunlight;
> With this spell and with this sign
> I pri'thee, forward my design.

Conjuring Three Fairies

By anointing your eyes with the following seventeenth-century potion, you could win a faery helper. The ointment had to be prepared in a house which the 'faries mayds doe use', however. A bucket of 'cleere water' was placed by the hearth there at the end of one day and collected again 'before the sonne ryse'. A surface scum like 'a whyte ryme like rawe milk or grease' was removed from the water with a silver spoon and put in a clean saucer. This was used to anoint the eyes and it enabled one to see 'thre fairye maydes', but only if the subject sat in a chair by the hearth the following night with his face towards the table, which had to be laid with three 'fyne loaves of new mangett, three newe knyves wyth whyte haftes and a new cuppe full of newe ale', all set upon a new towel. It was important to ignore the first faery, because she was 'malignant'. But the second or third faery could be caught and it would be possible to 'covenant with her for all matters convenient for your purpose', and she would always be with you.

BEWARE the DEAD

The faeries have long been associated with the dead. The most common site for faeryland was underground, which links it firmly with ideas of the Underworld and the lands of the dead.

Writing in the late seventeenth-century, Robert Kirk described faeries as unquiet departed spirits. According to his *Secret Commonwealth of Elves, Fauns and Faeries*, 'They also affirme thos Creatures that move invisibly in a House, and cast huge great Stones…to be Souls that have not attained their rest, thorough a vehement Desire of revealing a Murther or notable injurie done or received, or a Treasure that was forgot in their Liftyme on Earth, which when disclos'd to a Conjuror alone, the Ghost quite removes.'

Banshees

Many of the faeries of folk legend are described as death spirits. The Banshee of Ireland, traditionally foretold an impending death. A first-hand account of a Banshee encounter, while staying in a grand Irish home, was supplied by Lady Fanshawe (1625-76), in her *Memoirs*. The apparition of a woman with 'red hair and pale and ghastly complexion' awoke her at one o'clock in the morning. 'I was so much frightened, that my hair stood on end, and my night clothes fell off,' she recalled.

Lady Fanshawe was even more alarmed when her hostess told her the next morning that a member of her family had died that night and remarked that the shape of a woman traditionally appeared to people in the guest bedroom, each night that a family member lay dying in the house. Explaining the reason for the manifestation, she said: 'This woman was many ages ago got with child by the owner of this place, who murdered her in his garden and flung her into the river under the window.' Lady Fanshawe, quite understandably 'disposed to be gone suddenly' and returned to the safety of her own home.

Foolish Fire

The natural phenomenon of a flame-like phosphorescence flitting over marshy ground, sparked by gases from decaying vegetation, could account for the delusory Will-o'-the-wisp. However, *according to folk legend, it was the faeries at work. Further names for the malicious manifestation, include Jacky Lantern, Friar Rush, Kitty-candlestick, Hinky Punk and the Spunkies.*

The popular belief that the faeries were some class of the dead persisted in Ireland into the twentieth century. Recording a conversation with a countryman named John Graham, in *The Faery-Faith in Celtic Countries*, published in 1911, W. Y. Evans Wentz wrote: 'I now asked John what sort of a race the 'good people' are, and where they came from, and this is his reply: "People killed and murdered in war stay on earth till their time is up, and they are among the good people. The souls on this earth are as thick as the grass (running his walking stick through a thick clump), and you can't see them; and evil

spirits are just as thick, too, and people don't know it…The good people can see everything and you dare not meddle with them. They live in raths (tumuli) and their houses are in them. The opinion always was that they are a race of spirits, for they can go in different forms and can appear big as well as little."'

Further death spirits included the West Country Pixies, who some believed to be the spirits of unbaptized children. They enjoyed leading travellers astray, like the ghostly Will-o'-the-wisp faery, also known as Corpse Candle, when it was regarded as a death omen.

DREAM ON

FAERYLAND is the realm of the unconscious, a dream world in which anything can happen. 'A man can't always do what he likes, but he can fancy what he likes', the writer John Ruskin observed in an essay on 'Faeryland'.

Night-time is traditionally faery time. Fearful of light, the faery host vanishes by sunrise. Mortals may be visited by the faeries while they sleep, or be made to fall into an enchanted slumber by faery command. They may enter faeryland temporarily in dreams or trances, or for an indefinite period in the final 'sleep' of death.

Sleeping mortals could well find themselves at the mercy of the faeries. Folk legend and faery literature are full of such stories. Those who made the mistake of falling asleep on a faery mound were almost certain to be carried off to faeryland. It was rumoured that Robert Kirk, author of the seventeenth-century treatise *The Secret Commonwealth of Elves, Fauns and Fairies*, had been spirited away by the faeries, when he fell into a trance-like sleep, as a punishment for divulging their secrets in his book.

A popular medieval verse romance described King Orfeo's wife, Queen Meroudys, as falling asleep under a grafted apple tree, a plant with magical associations, and being carried off by the Faery King. She was returned but warned that she would be abducted the following night. Her husband ringed the tree with his soldiers, but the faery magic was too powerful. Queen Meroudys was drawn away invisibly from the centre of the ring. It was ten years before King Orfeo was able to win her back from faeryland.

The ancient belief that the soul goes out of the body in dreams, as in death, and meets the dead, is a recurrent motif in faery lore. An Irish tailor interviewed by W. Y. Evans Wentz for *The Fairy-Faith in Celtic Countries*, recalled a dream that had 'greatly disturbed' his father about a faery battle. The next morning 'an old woman who had the reputation of talking with the fairies' came to the house and described the dream to him. She was able to tell the man the names of some of the dream soldiers; they were the names of his friends who had died in battle.

NIGHTMARE COUPLINGS

THE FEARSOME faeries of folk legend were frequently the bringers of bad dreams. A nightmare was popularly believed to be caused by something heavy sitting on the sleeper's chest, many believing it must be an evil faery.

According to country superstition, these monsters of the night often coupled with the sleepers they visited. If they manifested themselves as a man, they were called an Incubus, if they were a woman, they were known as a Succubus, Nightmare or Hagge.

However, for the poet Geoffrey Chaucer, author of *The Wife of Bath's Tale*, it was more likely to be members of the Church rather than faeries that were up to no good. In a satirical jibe against lecherous friars in the tale, he wrote:

> Women may go safely up and down,
> In evry bush, or under evry tree
> There is none other incubus but he
> And he ne will doon them but dishonour.

It was generally agreed that taking a faery lover was a perilous matter. The seventeenth-century faerytale about the Bogy husband Bluebeard provides a chilling example. When his wife opens a locked room that she has been forbidden to enter, she finds a bloody chamber filled with the dead bodies of her many predecessors – a gruesome warning of her own impending doom.

Such a union was hedged around by rigid taboos. The mortal lover must never reveal the association, he must never reproach his faery mistress or visit her at any time not agreed by her, and certainly never touch her with any object made of iron. If he failed to meet any of these conditions, she would desert him immediately and he would never see her again. Any children they might have had would also be spirited away and never returned.

Sometimes the exacting pre-conditions proved too much and the match fell through. An old ballad called *The Elfin Knight* tells of a proposed union between Fair Isabel

and the Elfin Knight with an excessive pre-nuptial agreement: the faery required Isabel to make him a shirt of Holland linen without any cutting or needlework, which she must wash in a well 'where dew never wet nor rain ever fell', then dry on a hawthorn that had never budded. She, in turn, requested that he till an acre of her

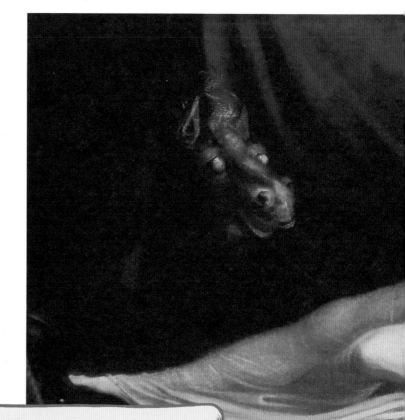

The artist Henry Fuseli was fascinated by the folk mythology of dream couplings. He was known as 'Principal Hobgoblin Painter to the Devil' because of his interest in the Incubus and Succubus, and painted several versions of an Incubus leaving two sleeping girls, in which the faery demon is pictured galloping away through an open window. His best known painting on the theme, The Nightmare, *is far more sinister. It portrays a hideous goblin Incubus seated on the stomach of a young woman sleeping in an attitude of surrender. A wild-eyed Night-Mare thrusts its head through the closed curtain.*

land with his horn, sow it with peppercorn, harrow it with a thorn and complete the work in one night. They agreed it would be easier not to proceed with the match, which was fortunate for Isabel, as her elfin knight then revealed he was already married and had seven children.

The Lennain Sith referred to by Kirk, also known as Leannan Sidhe, were faery variants of the immortal ladies of Celtic romance who lured men to their doom. The fourteenth-century story of Melusina, the monstrous daughter of a union between a mortal king and a faery, describes the pitfalls of such a mixed marriage, although, unusually, she appears to have suffered from the consequences as much as her husband.

Melusina was part woman, part monster. She was a serpent from the waist downwards, an infliction that happened periodically, until she married a man who promised never to see her on a Saturday. When all their children were born deformed in some way, her husband became suspicious and broke his promise. He saw his wife emerging serpent-like from her bath and subsequently shouted at her 'Get out of my sight, you pernicious snake! You have contaminated my children!' Melusina departed but returned to haunt the household as a Banshee.

SECOND SIGHT

century based on a survey he had undertaken. One correspondent revealed that James Mac Coilvicalaster, alias Grant, used to make room for invisible beings at his fireside: 'But whether the man saw any more than Brownie and Meg Mulloch, I am not very sure…others affirm he saw these two continually and sometimes many more.'

Those gifted with second sight could occasionally bestow the power on others. Sometimes contact with them was enough to make the faeries visible. Katharine Briggs recorded in *A Dictionary of Fairies* that Mrs Stewart, the wife of a minister in Edinburgh, had described such an experience to her. Mrs Stewart's father, his sister and another little boy, had been left with their grandmother for the day:

'Time went on and the children had begun perhaps to be a little troublesome to the old lady, when a friend came in whom they all liked and who had the reputation of having "the gift". She saw how things were and said: "Come with me and I'll show you something you'll like to see".' She made them hold hands to form a chain, and led them out into the gloaming. There was a little burn running past the cottage and a hillside beyond it. On the hillside a fire was burning and a circle of little people was dancing round it. The children gazed entranced until their friend led them back.'

Certain times of the year and of the day were better than others for seeing the faeries. Twilight, midnight and the hour before sunrise were considered the best times of day. The weather too should be taken into consideration according to Lewis Carroll in *Sylvie and Bruno*: 'The first rule is, that it must be a very hot day-that we may consider as settled.'

SOME PEOPLE did not need to resort to magic potions in order to see the faeries. Such mortals were known as 'second-sighted' in the Highlands, 'gifted' in England or 'sighted' in Ireland.

In *The Secret Commonwealth of Elves, Fauns and Fairies*, Robert Kirk described the torment of possessing such a power: 'He is not terrified with their Sight when he calls them, but seeing them in a surprise (as often he does) frightens him extreamly.'

John Aubrey published *An Accurate Account of Second Sighted Men in Scotland* in the seventeenth

Thomas the Rhymer

In the ancient ballad Thomas the Rhymer, Thomas is given clairvoyant powers by the Faery Queen when he places his head on her knee. He was in a fact a real man, a Scottish poet who lived in the thirteenth century. It was generally believed that he possessed second sight, and that he predicted the death of Alexander III of Scotland, the Battle of Bannockburn and the accession of James VI to the English throne.

He was reputed to have gained this prophetic knowledge from the Queen of Elfland, who fell in love with him, and carried him away to faeryland where she kept him captive for seven years. It was popularly believed that he returned to Faeryland when he died, and mortals who claimed to have visited Faeryland often reported seeing him there.

True Thomas lay oer yond grassy bank,
And he beheld a ladie gay,
A ladie that was brisk and bold,
Come riding over the fernie brae.

Her skirt was of the grass-green silk,
Her mantle of the velvet fine,
At ilka tett of her horse's mane
Hung fifty silver bells and nine.

NINETEENTH CENTURY VERSION OF *THE BALLAD OF TRUE THOMAS*

CAPTIVE in FAERYLAND

FAERY abductions of mortal adults were a
frequent and much feared occurrence,
often encountered in folk legend. If a
kidnapped man or woman made the mistake of
tasting faery food or drink, they generally could
not return for at least seven years, and when
they did, they generally degenerated into
solitary outcasts.

It was perilous to sleep outdoors at twilight,
particularly on a faery mound. A mortal was also
at risk of being snatched by the faeries if he
chanced to be wounded at twilight. Sir Walter
Scott expressed this belief in his early
nineteenth-century poem, *The Lady of the Lake*:

It was between the night and day,
When the Fairy King has power,
That I sunk down in a sinful fray
And 'twixt life and death was snatch'd away
To the joyless Elfin bower.

Women were generally in greater danger of being
snatched than men. Some were rescued but others,
sadly, were not, as in the tale of 'The Lothian
Farmer's Wife', included in *Scottish Fairy and Folk
Tales* by Sir George Douglas. The wife reappeared
after she had been abducted and explained to her
husband how he could win her back:

'The farmer, who ardently loved his wife, set out
on Hallowe'en, and, in the midst of a plot of
furze, waited impatiently for the
procession of the fairies. At the
ringing of the fairy bridles, and the
wild, unearthly sound which
accompanied the cavalcade, his heart
failed him, and he suffered the ghostly
train to pass by without interruption.
When the last had rode past, the
whole troop vanished, with loud
shouts of laughter and exultation;
among which he plainly discovered
the voice of his wife, lamenting that
he had lost her for ever.'

The farmer had not been brave
enough to win back his wife when
the faeries rode by with her. A
resourceful young woman, however,
in the ballad *Young Tam Lin*, was
more courageous in rescuing her
lover from a faery cavalcade. Intent
on freeing Tam Lin from his faery
enchantment, his sweetheart Janet
dragged him from his milk-white
steed and clung fast to him, even
though he metamorphosed into an
asp, an adder, a lion and a bolt of
red-hot iron. Finally, Tam Lin
changed into a 'mother-naked man'.

Changelings

The belief that faeries kidnapped mortal children and left a faery substitute in their place is a recurrent theme in folk legend. Various reasons were given for the practice: the theft of beautiful, golden-haired children was to improve the faery stock; abducted mortal children could be used instead of faery children as a tribute to Hell; or they could be set to work as servants.

When a child was born, every effort was made to prevent a faery abduction. The threat was at its greatest until the baby was christened or sometimes, just until it sneezed, and numerous spells or charms were employed to ward off faery kidnappers.

In some households, every cupboard and drawer would be locked '... for if care is not taken the faeries will get in and hide in the drawers and presses.' A live coal might be placed in the baby's first bath, while, when dressed, the infant was turned three times heels over head, blessed and then turned upside down and shaken three times.

Janet threw her green mantle over him, dipped him first in milk and then in hot water, and successfully removed the spell.

Mortals were often abducted by faeries for amorous reasons, but they were also taken away if they had a skill that the faeries desired. In *The Secret Rose*, W. B. Yeats included the tale of a young Irish schoolmaster, Red Hanrahan, who was wanted by the faeries for his learning and his songmaking. Hanrahan was lured onto a bare mountain one night and went through a door into faeryland:

'Every grand thing Hanrahan had ever heard of, and every colour he had ever seen was in it. There was sitting in a high chair a woman, the most beautiful the world ever saw, having a long pale face and flowers about it. And there were sitting on the step below her chair four grey old women, and one of them was holding a great cauldron in her lap; and another a great stone on her knees, and heavy as it was it seemed light to her; and another of them had a very long spear that was made of pointed wood; and the last of them had a sword that was without a scabbard.'

Hanrahan was informed that the four objects symbolized Pleasure, Power, Courage and Knowledge. The faeries waited for him to question them but he did not and they released him. He had been in faeryland for a year but it had passed in a night. He returned a broken man to discover that he had also lost the woman he had wanted to marry.

FAERY GODMOTHERS

A NEW FAERY character, the Faery Godmother, emerged with the publication of the first faery tales in England in the eighteenth century. The stories were based on folk themes but, unlike the faeries of traditional belief, the faery figures that featured in them were principally concerned with human morality.

The Faery Godmother is associated with blessing or punishment and the magic in the tales lies in people being shown to be what they really are. Surprise transformations are a frequent occurrence in the first faery stories; the beggar woman may be a faery, the frog may be a handsome prince, but they are essentially tests to prove the moral worth of the hero or heroine. The happy ending was never bestowed lightly, as the faery who had the power to make things go right made clear.

The evil spell cast by the old faery, angry because she had been overlooked by mistake and not invited to be a godmother to the princess in *The Sleeping Beauty*, echoes the ill-tempered behaviour of the faeries of folk legend. But the actions taken to thwart her by the young Faery Godmother who, fortunately, had yet to bestow her christening gift, establishes the new style

faery as a far superior moral being, who is still helps the mortals when the princess falls into her hundred years' sleep.

The Faery Godmother in *The Three Wishes*, first translated into English in the eighteenth century, underlined the fact that magic alone did not have the power to make people happy. A 'very beautiful Lady' appeared before a couple who believed their lives would be transformed if their wishes could come true. They were granted three wishes, but were unable to agree on what to wish for. They ended up with a yard-long black pudding, which was wished on to the wife's nose by mistake and had to be wished off with the final wish. Both agreed that their Faery Godmother had shown them the error of their ways.

The moral faeries of the classic faery tales reappeared in many of the stories produced in a creative outpouring of books for children towards the end of the nineteenth century. The illustrations for such books by gifted artists including Arthur Rackham, Edmund Dulac and Harry Clarke, ushered in a golden era of book illustration. This tradition has been continued by moderns artists such as Paul Raymond Gregory and Brian Froud.

In Cinderella, *the best known faery story, the heroine cannot be won by the prince until he has seen her in her true, humble state. Her Faery Godmother works her magic so that the prince falls in love with her but the hero has to prove his true worth by still wanting to marry her even when he discovers who she really is. In a translation of Charles Perrault's version of the story, the Faery Godmother exacts Cinderella's promise to be obedient, just as the faeries of folk legend might have done: '…her godmother, above all things, commanded her not to stay beyond twelve a clock at night; telling her at the same time, that if she stay'd at the ball one moment longer, her coach would be a pompion again, her horses mice, her footmen lizards, and her clothes resume their old form.'*

TIME TRAVEL

IME has no meaning in faeryland. A day there could be a year or a century to us. Occasionally, the opposite is true and a year in faeryland might be no more than a single mortal night.

In a Pembrokeshire tale, time in faeryland, unusually, passes in a flash. A young shepherd who joined a faery dance was carried off to faeryland. He spent many happy years there in a glittering palace surrounded by beautiful gardens but was warned never to drink from a fountain with silver and golden fish. Curiosity got the better of him, however, and he plunged his hands into the pool. Faeryland vanished and he found himself on a cold hillside among his sheep. Only minutes had passed since he joined the dance.

In general, time in faeryland was greatly accelerated, as mortals discovered to their cost when they returned. Walter Map, the twelfth-century author of *De Nugis Curialium*, provided one of the earliest examples of a faery time-lapse in the legend of King Herla, who journeyed into a subterranean faery world to fulfil a promise to a dwarf. The following version is from E. M. Leather's *The Folk-Lore of Herefordshire*:

'They entered a cave in a very high cliff, and after some journeying through the dark, which appeared to be lighted, not by the sun or moon, but by numerous torches, they arrived at the dwarf's palace, a splendid mansion.

There the marriage was celebrated, and the obligations to the dwarf fittingly paid, after which Herla returned home loaded with gifts

Fairy Time

Time in faeryland might differ from ours but the faeries were bound by mortal seasons. May Day, Midsummer Eve and Hallowe'en are considered the best days for seeing faeries or getting into faeryland, while twilight, midnight and full moon are the best times of the day. The days of the week are significant, too. Woe betide anyone who mentioned Sunday to a faery.

and offerings, horses, dogs, hawks and all things pertaining to hunting and falconry. The pigmy guided them down the dark passage, and there gave them a bloodhound small enough to be carried, then, strictly forbidding any of the king's retinue to dismount until the dog leapt from his carrier, he bade them farewell and returned home. Soon after, Herla reached the light of day, and having got news of his kingdom again, called an old shepherd and asked for news of his queen, using her name. The shepherd looked at him astonished, and said, "Lord, I scarcely understand your language, for I am a Saxon, and you a Briton. I have never heard of that queen, except in the case of one who they say was Herla's wife, queen of the earliest Britons. He is fabled to have disappeared with a dwarf at this cliff, and never to have been seen on earth again. The Saxons have now held this realm for two hundred years, having driven out the original inhabitants." The king was astonished, for he imagined that he had been away for three days only.'

Herla's time travel left him a broken man, a perpetual wanderer with no home to go to. Rip Van Winkle had a similar shock when he awoke, following a trip to faeryland, to discover that his dog had gone and that his firearm was heavy with rust. He made his way back home, only to discover that the house was deserted and all his former friends had gone. He had apparently slept for twenty years. According to Washington Irving, the author of *Rip Van Winkle*, the story of his famous character, a happy-go-lucky hen-pecked husband, was originally recounted by Diedrich Knickerbocker. Rip Van Winkle set out on his enchanted journey as a subject of George III, and returned as a free citizen of the United States.

When Einion in the Welsh legend was allowed to return home for a while, on condition he went back to faeryland, he found: 'not one of his people or old friends knew him. Everybody believed that he had been killed by another shepherd. And this shepherd had been accused of the murder and fled to America.'

FAERYLAND in VICTORIAN ART

IT WAS not until the turn of the eighteenth century that the faeries were taken up with any real seriousness by British artists, by which time there was a vast body of faery literature to draw upon. It was soon apparent that such subject matter had enormous visual appeal and, by the mid-nineteenth century, not only had faery painting emerged as a distinct art genre, it was also enjoying a considerable vogue.

An insular spirit prevailed in the Victorian age, which helped to make faery paintings more popular. Shakespeare was revered as a great British writer and paintings inspired by themes from his plays were very fashionable. His concept of a faeryland somewhere at the heart of the British countryside was underlined by nineteenth-century artists, who helped to create an image of the faeries in art as representatives of the British folk heritage.

More importantly, the popularity of faery paintings was a reaction against the prevailing utilitarianism of the times. It was a celebration of magic in a period predominantly concerned with establishing facts. Mystery was increasingly edged aside in a search for the kind of certitude afforded by experimental science, and the postulation of an imaginary other world in art was an assertion of the fantastic and irrational during a period of spiritual duress.

Appropriately, it was a Celt, Sir Joseph Noel Paton, who was one of the best-known Victorian faery painters. Paton's epic scenes from *A Midsummer Night's Dream*, based on the quarrel and reconciliation of Oberon and Titania, caused a popular sensation when they were first

exhibited. He went further than any previous artist in the detailed depiction of the diminutive faery world, and his paintings contain a riot of faery activity on the tiniest scale. In Paton's microscopic faeryland, a bubble could double as a faery boat and a spider turn into a gigantic monster. The public loved his crowded faery scenes.

Paton's meticulously delineated faerylands exhibit a Pre-Raphaelite attention to detail, but when the leading Pre-Raphaelite painter Sir John Everett Millais ventured into faeryland with his painting *Ferdinand Lured by Ariel*, the effect was very different. The almost photographic realism with which Millais depicted Ferdinand and his leafy surroundings, made his faeryland a much more believable vision. His unidealized hovering Ariel with a flying escort of bat-like faery attendants was a far cry from the decorative faery extravaganzas painted by Paton and others, and it shocked the public. The dealer who had commissioned the painting refused the finished work, complaining of the 'greenness of the fairies'.

Millais' view of faeryland was a departure from the popular mainstream. Another Victorian artist who provided an alternative vision that was even more extraordinary was the committed faery painter, Richard Dadd. He painted one of the most haunting images of faeryland, *The Fairy Feller's Master-Stroke*, in Bethlehem Hospital asylum, where he was confined after murdering his father. The picture is an incredibly detailed, almost hallucinogenic vision of a tiny world within the heart of the British countryside. It took Dadd nine years to complete.

FAERY PHOTOGRAPHS

THE VICTORIAN fascination with other worlds, manifested in the vogue for faery painting, was also evident in the increased popularity of spiritualism in the nineteenth century.

A craze for recording the paranormal in 'spirit' photography sprang up. The first such image was taken in 1862 by an American photographer, William Mumler. Spirit photography flourished in Britain from the mid-1870s to the turn of the century. Faery photography was the logical extension of these investigations. The publication of a series of pictures of faeries taken by two girls in a Yorkshire village in 1917 and 1920 aroused huge public interest. Two of the faery photographs were first published in the Christmas edition of the *Strand Magazine* in 1920, in an article by Sir Conan Doyle and Edward Gardner entitled 'An

Epoch-making Event – Fairies Photographed'. The issue was sold out in three days and the story taken up by newspapers around the world.

The photographs were dubbed the 'Cottingley Fairy Photographs', because they had been taken by the two girls, Elsie Wright and her cousin Frances Griffiths in Cottingley Glen. They showed Frances and Elsie with dancing faeries and 'Fairies and their Sun-Bath'. The first two, taken in 1917, when Elsie was 16 and Frances 10, were sent to Mr Gardner, an experienced investigator of the paranormal. Suspicious that they were fakes, he requested the glass negatives and showed them to a professional photographer, who said they had not been faked: 'I don't know anything about fairies,' Mr Gardner later reported him as saying, 'but these photographs are straight, open-air, single-exposure shots.' Mr Gardner sought a second opinion from Kodak, who also said there was no sign of the photographs being faked. Kodak refused to issue a certificate of genuineness, however, 'because photography lent itself to a multitude of processes, and some clever operator might have made them artificially'.

Intrigued, Mr Gardner met Elsie and went to the glen with her. She told him she had 'seen and played with fairy creatures since she could remember anything, and actually to photograph them did not appeal to her as being very extraordinary'. Mr Gardner was impressed by her sincerity and decided both girls must be clairvoyants. But he needed more proof and so he arranged for twenty-four secretly marked glass plates to be made. He then gave these to the girls and asked for further faery photographs.

Three more faery photographs taken in the glen, were duly supplied in 1920 and they showed no signs of being fakes. They were also published in the *Strand Magazine*, adding further fuel to the national debate raging as to whether they possibly could be genuine. Faery

supporters received fresh ammunition in 1922 when Conan Doyle defended the photographs in his book *The Coming of the Fairies*.

The arrival of the clairvoyant Geoffrey Hodson on the scene in 1921 was an additional bonus. He settled down in the glen with the girls to await developments. Almost immediately, he recorded in *Fairies at Work and Play*, published in 1925, they were 'surrounded by a dancing group of lovely female fairies'. His attention was riveted by the faery leader, 'a female figure, probably two feet high, surrounded by transparent flowing drapery'.

Experts now agree that the faery figures in the Cottingley photographs were painted cut-outs. There is evidence to prove that Elsie showed considerable talent for drawing and painting, particularly of faeries. She continued to maintain that they were genuine photographs of faeries, however. 'I've told you that they're photographs of figments of our imagination and that's what I'm sticking to,' she said, when interviewed in 1971.

Exposed!

Following the magazine articles and the book, Conan Doyle and Edward Gardner were deluged with letters from people around the world who claimed to have seen faeries. A faery photograph was sent in, that claimed to be a genuine picture of a little brownie at the foot of a tree. 'When however our usual photographic analysis was made,' Mr Gardner reported, 'the figure of the brownie showed up at once as a clever artificial structure. When the author was challenged with this evidence he admitted the fact and excused the attempt by saying that he wished to prove that deception was possible by the use of built-up figures.

MODERN MASTER: BRIAN FROUD

THE RECENT revival of interest in faery themes has meant that a new era of fantasy illustration is emerging. Spearheading the renaissance is British artist Brian Froud, whose lavishly illustrated book of British faery lore, *Faeries*, produced with fellow artist Alan Lee, became a best-seller on both sides of the Atlantic. Froud's most recent publications are *Lady Cottington's Pressed Fairy Book* and *Good Faeries/Bad Faeries*.

Froud's deep involvement with folklore was triggered when he was a student and first discovered the splendid faery illustrations of the British artist Arthur Rackham, whose work had brought a new imaginative grace to faeryland. Froud went on to develop his own distinctive vision, which also found its way onto film. He created the fantasy otherworlds celebrated in two popular feature films by Jim Henson, *The Dark Crystal* and *Labyrinth*.

Froud aims to go beyond mainstream illustration, and has described his pictures as being: 'In the oral tradition, where stories are told around the fireplace in semi-darkness, the words are alive; they leave the lips, enter into the air, and before they fall onto your ear, they transform themselves into magic. They're not fixed; they change from telling to telling, and from listener to listener. I want my pictures to have that same quality of mutability. I don't want things to be fixed too solidly or explained too fully; I want each viewing to be like the retelling of a tale, full of new possibilities.'

Striving to show a sense of the supernatural within everyday realism, he combines fantastical elements with ordinary imagery to make them believable, although he is careful to maintain a certain vagueness and sense of mystery. Froud has said, 'I find that some of the fantasy genre painters tend to over-paint their pictures. The artist has finished every detail, and every edge is hard and bright – which does not allow me into their world, my eye slides off that shiny surface.'

Picture Acknowledgements

Alan Lee 10, 11, 24, 51, 61(br)

Brian Froud 3, 5(bl), 6, 8(br), 18 (bl), 21, 28, 49, 50(b), 51, 52, 53(l), 54/55, 68(bl), 69(br), 72(t), 77, 83, 85, 92, 93

Richard Doyle, *In Fairyland* (1870), 16/17, 18(tl), 20(bl), 22(bl), 32/33, 38(t), 45, 57, 96

Cover, 64/65 John Anster Fitzgerald, *The Fairies' Banquet*, Maas Gallery/Bridgeman Art Library (BAL); 2 J.G. Gregory, *A Flower Fairy*, Fine Art Photographic Library Ltd (FAPL); 7 Arthur Rackham, *A Fairy Song*, Spencer Collection, New York Public Library/BAL; 8 John Anster Fitzgerald, *The Captive Robin*, Christie's Images/BAL; 9 Edmund Dulac, *Nocturnal Spires*, Victoria & Albert Museum/BAL; 11(tl) Charles Prosper Sainton, *Fen Fairy*, Maas Gallery/BAL; 12(l) Maud Tindal Atkinson, *Ariel*, Private collection (PC); 13(br) C. Wilhelm, *Robin Goodfellow*, Victoria & Albert Museum/BAL; 14/15 Edward Robert Hughes, *Twilight Fantasies*, Maas Gallery/BAL; 16 Arthur Rackham, *The Country of Enchantment*, Sotheby's; 19(r) Margaret Tarrant, *Fairies Midst Sweet Peas*, PC/BAL; 20(t) Thomas Heatherley, *Fairy Seated on a Mushroom*, PC/BAL; 22(t) *Fairy Ring*, Mary Evans Picture Library (ME); 23 Edward Robert Hughes, *Midsummer Eve*, Maas Gallery/BAL; 25 William Robert Symonds, *The Princess and the Frog*, Bradford Art Galleries & Museums/BAL; 26 Eleanor Fortescue-Brickdale, *Prospero and Ariel*, Chris Beetles Ltd/BAL; 27(b) Rowland Wheelwright, *The Enchanted Shore*, Sotheby's; 28 Claude Shepperson, *A Spell for a Fairy*, ME; 29 Arthur Rackham, *The Fairy's Tightrope*, PC/BAL; 30(tl) Ernst Stohr, *An Autumn Fairy Tale*, Sotheby's; 30(br) H.J. Ford, *A Giant's Shadow*, ME; 31 Arthur Rackham, *Sprite and Monster*, Chris Beetles Ltd/BAL; 33(t) Amelia Jane Murray, *A Fairy Resting on a Shell*, Christie's Images; 34/35 Helen Jacobs, *The Night Flight*, PC/BAL; 35 Ernest Aris, *Thistledown Elves*, ME; 36/37 Arthur Rackham, *Twilight Dreams*, University of Liverpool Art Gallery & Collections/BAL; 38(br) C. Wilhelm, *Bottom*, Victoria & Albert Museum/BAL; 39 John Anster Fitzgerald, *The Concert*, Christie's Images; 40 Sir Joseph Noel Paton, *The Quarrel of Oberon and Titania* (detail), National Gallery of Scotland/BAL; 40/41 Richard Dadd, *Contradiction: Oberon and Titania*, FAPL; 42/43 Sir Joseph Noel Paton, *The Reconciliation of Oberon and Titania*, National Gallery of Scotland/BAL; 44/45 Henry Meynell Rheam, *The Fairy Wood*, Roy Miles Gallery/BAL; 46 Thomas Heatherley, *Fairy Resting on a Mushroom*, PC; 47 John Simmons, *Titania Lying on a Leaf*, Maas Gallery/BAL; 48 Henry Meynell Rheam, *Queen Mab*, Fine Art Society/BAL; 50(l) Arthur Rackham, *A House Plagued by Goblins*, PC; 53(r) Arthur Rackham, *Goblins Tempting a Girl with their Fruit*, PC; 54 George Cruikshank, *The Elves and the Shoemaker*, ME; 55 F. Richardson, *Fairies Weaving the Magic Cloak*, Images; 56 Beatrice Goldsmith, *Watching the Fairies*, Chris Beetles Ltd/BAL; 58/59 Charles Altamont Doyle, *A Dance Around the Moon*, Maas Gallery/BAL; 60 Arthur Rackham, *Fairies Making Music*, PC; 61(tl) Arthur Rackham, *Ferdinand Hears the Fairy Music*, PC; 62(t) Ida Rentoul Outhwaite, *Fairies Dancing*, Chris Beetles Ltd/BAL; 62(l) Walter Jenks Morgan, *Where Rural Fays and Fairies Dwell*, PC/BAL; 63 Arthur Rackham, *Dancing with the Fairies*, PC/BAL; 64(tl) Arthur Rackham, *An Elf Attendant on Bottom*, Private collection/BAL; 65(br) Arthur Rackham, *The Elves' Party*, PC; 66/67 Sir Joseph Noel Paton, *The Fairy Raid*, Glasgow Art Gallery & Museum/BAL; 68/69 John Anster Fitzgerald, *The Fairy's Funeral*, Maas Gallery/BAL; 70 Sir Hubert von Herkomer, *Bottom Asleep*, PC/BAL; 70/71 Edmund Dulac, illustration from *Beauty and the Beast*, Victoria & Albert Museum/BAL; 71 John Anster Fitzgerald, *Fairies Looking through a Gothic Arch* (detail), PC/BAL; 72(b) Anon, *An Irish Banshee*, ME; 73 Arthur Hughes, *Jack O'Lantern*, Christie's Images/BAL; 74/75 John Anster Fitzgerald, *The Stuff that Dreams are Made Of*, PC/BAL; 76(t) Francis Barrett, *Head of Asmodeus*, PC/BAL; 76/77 Henry Fuseli, *The Nightmare*, Detroit Institute of Arts/BAL; 78 Eleanor Fortescue-Brickdale, *The Introduction*, Phillips/BAL; 79 Sir Joseph Noel Paton, *La Belle Dame Sans Merci (The Story of Thomas Rhymer)*, Roy Miles/BAL; 80(t) Arthur Rackham, *Fairy Stealing a Child*, PC; 80(b) Arthur Rackham, *Fairies Peep at a Baby*, PC; 81 Warwick Goble, *Fairies Provide a Human Girl with Fairy Wings*, ME; 82 Arthur Rackham, *Cinderella with her Fairy Godmother*, PC; 84 Arthur Rackham, *Rip Van Winkle's Sleep*, PC; 86 Sir John Everett Millais, *Ferdinand Lured by Ariel*, The Makins Collection/BAL; 87 Richard Dadd, *The Fairy Feller's Master-stroke*, Tate Gallery, London; 88/89 John Anster Fitzgerald, *The Fledgling*, Maas Gallery/BAL; 90 Frances Griffiths and the Cottingley Fairies, ME; 91(bl) Cottingley fairy photograph, Images Colour Library; 91(br) Photograph of Sir Arthur Conan Doyle, ME; 94 Richard Doyle, *Asleep in the Moonlight*, British Library/BAL